The Yellow Leaves

The Yellow Leaves
A Miscellany

Frederick Buechner

Westminster John Knox Press
LOUISVILLE • LONDON

Book design by Drew Stevens
Cover design by designpointinc.com

First edition
Published by Westminster John Knox Press
Louisville, Kentucky

This book is printed on acid-free paper that meets the American National Standards Institute Z39.48 standard. ⊛

PRINTED IN THE UNITED STATES OF AMERICA

08 09 10 11 12 13 14 15 16 — 10 9 8 7 6 5 4 3 2 1

Library of Congress Cataloging-in-Publication Data

Buechner, Frederick, 1926–
    The yellow leaves : a miscellany / Frederick Buechner.—1st ed.
        p. cm.
    ISBN 978-0-664-23276-4 (alk. paper)
    1. Buechner, Frederick, 1926– 2. Novelists, American—20th century—Biography.
3. Presbyterian Church—Clergy—Biography. I. Title.
    PS3552.U35Z475 2008
    813'.54—dc22
    [B]
                                                                    2007046592

In memory of Michael Mayne
and with love to his wife, Alison

Contents

Introduction

That time of year thou mayst in me behold
When yellow leaves, or none, or few, do hang
Upon those boughs which shake against the cold,
Bare ruined choirs where late the sweet birds sang.
                                        —William Shakespeare

I can still write sentences and paragraphs, but for some five or six years now I haven't been able to write books. Maybe after more than thirty of them the well has at last run dry. Maybe, age eighty, I no longer have the right kind of energy. Maybe the time has simply come to stop. Whatever the reason, at least for the moment the sweet birds no longer sing.

On the other hand, during this unproductive time I started a number of things which for one reason or another I decided to leave unfinished but which, on rereading, I decided maybe had enough life in them to warrant inclusion in a volume like this. A story, some reminiscences, a handful of poems about my family, a scene from a novel—they are the yellow leaves that hang upon these boughs that are not so bare and ruined but that they still dream from time to time of the sweet birds' return.

Our Last Drive Together

It was while my mother was staying with us in Vermont that the fatal phone call came. It was from Incoronata, the woman who for years had been her factotum and mainstay in the New York apartment that she rarely left except for occasional visits to us or trips to the doctor or the hearing aid people who were always selling her new models, none of which, she said, were any damn good.

Incoronata must have spent hours working herself up to it because I'd barely lifted the receiver when she dropped her bombshell. She said she was quitting. She said she'd had all she could take. She said there was nothing more to say. And then she said a good deal more.

She told me my mother said such terrible things to her that I wouldn't believe it if she repeated them. She said she had to work like a slave and never got a word of thanks for it, let alone any time off. She said her live-in boyfriend threatened to walk out on her if she stayed on the job a day longer because in her present state she was giving him ulcers. She was getting ulcers herself, she said. And no wonder. She said she had left the key to the apartment with one of the doormen because she would not be needing it again to let herself in. And that was that. She said she was on the verge of a nervous breakdown.

I could feel my scalp run cold at the thought of my mother's reaction and said everything I could think of to make Incoronata change her mind. I told her my mother was devoted to her no matter what terrible things she said. I told her the whole family was devoted to her. I told her that when people got old and deaf and started falling to pieces, they said things they didn't mean and then felt awful about it afterward. I said I didn't know how my mother could possibly manage without her, how any of us could. I said we would give her a raise and see to it that she got more time off. But by then she was so close to hysterics I don't think she even heard me.

So I changed my tactics and begged her at least to stay on till we could find somebody to replace her, at least to be there when we got back from Vermont to help my mother unpack and get resettled. But if she did that, Incoronata said, she knew my mother would find some way to make her stay, and with her nerves the way they were she simply couldn't face it. So there was nothing more to say, and we finally hung up.

The question then became how to break the news to Kaki, which was what her grandchildren called my mother as eventually all of us did. To have told her then and there would have been to ruin the rest of her visit for all of us, so we decided to wait till I had managed to find somebody else to replace her and then not breathe a word till we had gotten her back to her apartment where there would be another Incoronata waiting to welcome her and she would simply have to accept the new state of things as a fait accompli.

My brother Jamie, who lived in New York too, came up by bus to help with the historic drive back. There was the usual mound of luggage piled out on the lawn—the suitcases with bits of brightly colored yarn tied around their handles to identify them, the plastic and canvas carry-alls, the paper shopping bags from Saks and Bonwits stuffed with things like her hair dryer, her magnifying mirror, extra slippers, and so on. There was the square Mark Cross case she kept her jewelry in and the flowered duffel bag with her enormous collection of pills and assorted medicines together with a second like it which was full of all the things she needed for making up her face in the morning. She said it was all of it breakable so for God's sake not to put anything heavy on it and to be sure to put her long black garment bag in at the very end so it could lie flat on top of everything else and her best clothes wouldn't end up a mass of wrinkles.

We put her white plastic toilet seat extender behind her on the back seat like a wedding cake in case she needed it on the way. She kept her straw purse on her lap with things she might want during the journey like her smelling salts and Excedrin and the little flask of water in case she started to choke. She also had me put a can of root beer in the cup holder because she said root beer was the only thing that helped her dry throat. The final thing was to get Jamie to stuff her little velvet, heart-shaped pillow in behind the small of her back because she said he was the only one who knew how to do it properly.

She had one of her many chiffon scarves around her neck to keep off drafts and another one, just for looks, tied around her melon-shaped straw hat with her crescent-shaped diamond pin to hold it in place. For shoes she wore her usual suede Hush Puppies with crepe soles to prevent her from slipping and kept her cane within reach at her side. Before we started off I told her not to forget to fasten her seat belt, but she refused. She said she sat so low in her seat that the strap went across her face and almost knocked her dentures out, and that got all three of us laughing so hard I was able to click it into place without her even noticing.

Driving with Kaki was one of the best ways there was of visiting with her because with no other noises to distract her I could speak in my normal voice, and that meant that not only could we speak the kinds of things that can't be shouted but could do it like the old friends we were instead of the carica-tures we became when almost nothing I said got through to her. Heading west through the rolling green farmland, I began to think of her again as the hero she had been all through my childhood when it seemed there was nothing she couldn't do, no company she couldn't charm, no disaster she couldn't pull us all through like my father's death in a garage filled with bitter blue fumes when I was ten and Jamie going on eight. I remembered how proud I was of how much younger and prettier and funnier she was than the mothers of any of my friends and how I loved being with her. I remembered the new life she had made for us in Bermuda in a pink house called the Moorings on the harbor across from Hamilton where Jamie and I could catch fish much too beautiful to keep and where we lived until 1939 when the war broke out and we had to go home.

At sixty miles an hour she seemed as mobile as I was, and I couldn't imagine her ever again having to hand herself across a room from chair back to chair back groaning that her knees bent the wrong way like a stork's and she had no balance and couldn't imagine what in God's name was wrong with her. What was wrong with her, of course, was that she would be ninety on her next birthday, but if ever I tried telling her that, she would put her hands over her ears and close her eyes tight shut. Sometimes she would scream.

Jamie was dozing in the back seat next to the toilet seat extender, and all was peaceful until she complained that the sun was getting in her eyes and giving her a terrible headache. She had her dark glasses on, but she said they were no damn good so I pulled her sun visor down, and she said any fool could see she was too low in her seat for that to be any damn good either. She told me to stop at the next service station we came to and get her a piece of cardboard or something to cover her half of the windshield. I explained if I did that I wouldn't be able to see the road properly, and she said she couldn't believe a man would treat his own mother the way I did.

Her next step was to take off the chiffon scarf she had around her neck and get Jamie to tie it on from behind like a blindfold. That seemed to work at first, but then she said she needed something heavier so he took off his jacket and draped it over the melon-shaped hat and the chiffon scarf. We said it made her look as if she was being kidnapped by terrorists, and she said we could laugh all we wanted, but as for her she failed to see the joke.

Not long afterward she said in a muffled voice that she was having trouble breathing. If it led to a heart attack, she supposed that would give us another good chuckle. But by this time we weren't driving into the sun anymore, so Jamie took off her various wrappings, and for a while she didn't say anything until we hit a stretch of rough pavement. Each time the car gave the smallest jounce, she sucked her breath in through her teeth like a hissing radiator. It was like me, she said, to pick out the worst road I could find when I knew what it did to her back.

It was toward the end of the journey as we were barreling down the Hudson River Parkway toward the Seventy-ninth Street exit that she told me she had to get to a bathroom in a hurry. I told her there was no way in the world we could find her a bathroom where we were, but if she could just hold out about twenty minutes longer, we would have her home. She told me she never dreamed that the child she'd almost died giving birth to would treat her like a dog the way I did, and it was at that point that I found myself having fantasies. I could pull the car over to the side of the road and just leave her there with all her belongings including the seat extender. I could move to another country. I could grow a beard and change my name.

She did hold out, as it happened, but by the time the doorman had helped her out of the car and into the elevator, she was in such a rush she didn't even notice that it wasn't Incoronata who opened the door to let us in. When she eventually came out of the bathroom, she still had her hat on her head with one end of the chiffon scarf trailing out behind her, and it was only then that she noticed that the person who was offering to take it off for her was a total stranger.

As briefly and calmly as I could, I explained what had happened to Incoronata, and to my surprise she didn't explode the way I'd been dreading but just stood there in the hallway looking old and dazed with her skirt pulled crooked. Incoronata's replacement, whose name turned out to be Sheila, was under five feet tall, and it wasn't until she had helped her lie down on her bed and taken her shoes off that Kaki spoke to her for the first time.

"Get me a root beer out of the icebox," she barked and then, before Sheila left the bedroom, "That dyed hair doesn't fool me for a minute. She's seventy if she's a day. And if you think I'm going to have a dwarf taking care of me, you're out of your minds."

Kaki's bedroom was where she spent the last few years of her life, rarely leaving it except when Jamie and his wife came for supper. She had pasted gold stars on almost everything—the headboard of her bed, the picture frames, the lamp shades, the covers of books. Her chaise longue was heaped with pillows, and there was a pile of magazines on the carpet beside it and a fake leopard-skin throw at the foot. There was her bow-fronted antique desk that she loved telling she'd bought out from under the nose of a childhood friend who would have killed for it, and the dressing table where she used to do her face the first thing every morning until she took to having the powder and lipstick and eyebrow pencil and what have you brought to her on a tray while she was still in bed.

The glass-topped green bureau was loaded with colognes, hairsprays, eyedrops, cough syrup. There was a jar of almonds that she had read kept you from getting cancer and a bowl of M&M's that she said gave her energy. A number of pictures hung on the peach-colored walls including a watercolor of the Moorings with its whitewashed roof and the blue harbor beyond it. She said she'd never been so happy anywhere else. There was a framed piece of needlepoint she'd done with the word "JOY" on it and several ladybugs for luck. She kept her bedside telephone under a quilted tea cozy and beside it a little covered china dish for her teeth at night.

It was in this room that early one morning she died in her sleep. Little pint-sized Sheila was the one who phoned Jamie the news. He said that when he got to the apartment shortly afterward, she told him she had put one of Kaki's best nighties on her and the ribboned pink bedjacket that was her favorite.

She had washed her face and hands and brushed her hair. When he turned to go in and see her, Sheila went and busied herself with something in the kitchen.

Kaki was lying on her bed with a fresh sheet pulled up all the way over her. He said that for a few moments he thought he would pull it back to have one last look at her face and then didn't. He just stood at the window for a while staring down at Seventy-ninth Street three stories below. The windowsill felt gritty to his touch. He noticed that one of the muslin curtains needed mending.

When the long black vehicle with side curtains pulled up at the awninged front entrance, he found himself remembering an exchange he and I had had with her once. She had told us for God's sake not to let them carry her out in a bag when the time came, and we had told her we wouldn't. Instead, I said, I would take her under one arm and Jamie would take her under the other and together we would walk her out between us, which had gotten all three of us laughing the way we did in the car when she said the seat belt strap almost knocked her dentures out.

Down below he could see the undertakers talking to the doorman. He went back and stood by the bed for a few moments, then reached down under the bottom of the sheet and pinched one of her toes.

"They're coming," he said.

Johnny

My wife's brother, Johnny, spent years of his life doing wooden puzzles with pieces he could take out and put back again. Sometimes he got the elephant-shaped piece back into its elephant-shaped place on the first try or turned it this way and that way with his long delicate fingers until it fitted. Other times he held it suspended in the air so long that his arm finally sank down to the table. Either way, his face always wore the same look of disdain. It was like the face of a man cleaning up a dog mess—his lips pursed, his eyebrows raised, to distance himself as far as he could.

The men who took care of him kept the TV going all day long, but he seemed to pay no attention to it. He seemed to pay no attention either to the wide stretch of inland waterway he could see through the picture window he faced from his wheelchair, its banks dotted with one-story houses like his, each with a screened-in pool and a dock and a palm tree or two. There was always a lot going on to watch—speedboaters, waterskiers, people fishing, swimming, sunbathing but he appeared either not to notice it or to be bored by it.

If you hadn't known better you might have taken him for a

Supreme Court justice. He had a grave, unlined face, and thick dark hair and dark eyebrows. His mouth was small and shapely like the mouth of a silent movie star.

In his earlier days he had talked a little. If you pointed to things in a picture book—a fire engine, an ice cream cone, a pussy cat—he could name them in a blurred sort of way as if he had no roof to his mouth, but in time he either lost the ability or just didn't feel like it. Ralph, who had taken care of him for thirty years or more—a short, fat man with warts on his eyelids and a knack for picking winners at Saratoga—could sometimes get him to repeat things after him like "Thank you" or "Mother," but there were only two things I can remember ever having heard him say on his own.

One of them was Nowanna. The van was ready to take him for a drive. Nowanna. They were going to lower him into the swimming pool in his canvas sling. Nowanna. If he wanted dessert, he had to finish his spaghetti first. It was time to go to the bathroom. His sister had come with birthday presents. Nowanna, nowanna, nowanna. Sometimes he groaned it. Sometimes he bellowed it like a cow in labor. Sometimes it rose at the end to a desperate, ear-splitting crescendo. You wanted to strangle him. Sometimes it was how he greeted his mother when he saw her coming through the door.

The other thing was Please. He would suddenly reach out his hand to you and say it—Please, Please—as if his life depended on it. As if his life depended on you. His silky, cool hand would go limp in yours. Then, slow as a lemur, he would withdraw it. He would turn his head away with a look of vague embarrassment. "Please," he would say. As if his heart would break if you didn't.

His parents moved heaven and earth, of course, at least his mother did. His father felt so helpless and uncomfortable in his presence, he left it mainly to her. Doctor after doctor was consulted. They experimented with medications that would control his epileptic seizures without turning him into a zombie and other medications for other things that were wrong with him. "Doubly disabled" was the term they used for him: physically because he couldn't do lots of things other people could and psychologically because it depressed the hell out of him. So they tried other medications for the depression, some that worked better than others, some that made matters only worse. They also tried placing him temporarily in various sanatoriums and mental hospitals, always making sure that he had a suite of rooms to himself with nurses around the clock, but once he was settled in one of them, the visits of doctors and therapists tended to become fewer and fewer. Nobody seemed interested in new ways to get him to walk and talk. If he was going to find a way to join the human race, he was going to have to find it on his own.

The next step was to establish him in a house of his own with Ralph and three or four others who took turns looking after him and a woman to cook and clean. The hope was that it would be less stressful than having him at home and might also encourage him toward some sort of independence. His mother saw to it that he was surrounded by things she thought appropriate to a young man his age—leather armchairs, sporting prints, athletic equipment, framed photographs of his family and of himself while he was still able to kick a ball around and rake leaves—and gradually she and the others ascribed to him a personality to go with it. They joked about him as a kind of amiable eccentric—cantankerous, demanding, unpredictable but as good-hearted inwardly as he was unresponsive outwardly. Above all he was treated as the master of his own house. Ralph took to calling him Tiger, and everybody was instructed to say "Mr. Merck's residence" when they answered his phone.

None of it worked. Not only was he unable so much as to dream of kicking a ball or raking leaves again, but it reached the point where he could walk only with somebody to support him under each arm moaning nowanna as he went, and it became such a hassle to get him to use a knife and fork at meals that they took to feeding him themselves so regularly that for a while he lost the ability to do it on his own.

Somewhere along the line his mother found her way to a

powerhouse of a Christian Science practitioner called Sunny. She specialized in women of means whom she referred to as her "convertibles" and had Mary Baker Eddy shelved in her office next to a business encyclopedia and a guide to investing. My clearest picture of her is the way she appeared at our wedding with her hair in a pompadour, a hat with a plume in it, and a veil drawn tight over her triangular face and sharp little eyes. She looked like the bad fairy at the christening.

By the sheer force of her personality she helped my mother-in-law survive. Since God was perfect, she explained, everything God made must obviously be perfect too including Johnny. He was God's perfect child and to see him as anything else was only an Error of Mortal Mind. She must keep on telling him that he was God's perfect child and, more important still, she must keep on telling herself. She must *know* it. And Sunny herself would be working on him as well, she said. She never said praying for him—I suppose because that implied there was something real to pray about—but working on him in the sense of *knowing* until the sweat trickled down from under her veil that he was as perfect an example of God's creation as the lily in the field.

"If I didn't know that someday Johnny is going to be well," his mother said to me once, "I wouldn't want to go on living." But with another part of herself that strong, good woman knew as clearly as anybody else that there wasn't a chance in the world of his ever being anything but the one who sat there year after year with his feet in their white cotton socks flopping out over the edge of his wheelchair as useless as flippers. Nevertheless, for the rest of her life she studied *Science and Health* every morning before they brought in her breakfast tray; and when to her horror Sunny committed the final Error by dying like everybody else, she found various other practitioners to take her place. But all of it was so clearly in vain that added to her grief was a terrible burden of guilt. If only she could do it *right*. If only she could see him as the perfect child she tried so hard to know he was.

As for me, I caught two different glimpses. One was in a

dream that for years I kept on dreaming. Johnny and I would be together somewhere, just the two of us. The storm had somehow passed, the battle had somehow been won, and we were looking back on it. I remember the enormous relief we both felt that everything had finally worked out. Like old war comrades talking about the war, we talked about how sad and terrible it had been. We talked about how wonderful it was now. I told him how wonderful it was to be able to talk to him, to hear him talking like everybody else. I felt enormously close to him, enormously happy that after all the lost years he was at last my friend and true brother.

The other glimpse was his smile. It was as unpredictable as it was rare, but one thing that sometimes prompted it was the only joke I ever knew him to play. My wife's name is Judy and her sister's is Bambi, but sometimes when Judy and I went to see him together, he would stretch his hand out to her and call her Bambi, knowing full well that he was doing it wrong. It was a smile that transformed his whole face but so slowly and subtly that like the rising of the sun you were hardly aware what was happening until the whole room was flooded with light. It was a smile of such radiance that it somehow canceled out everything that was not radiant—everything about him, everything about us, everything about life. It was the smile of Columbus sighting the New World. It was the lost colony of Atlantis rising out of the waves.

There was no way of knowing what he wanted when he reached out as far as his arm would stretch, but in case what he wanted was me, I always took his hand in mine. Then, invariably, he would turn his head and look the other way as if I wasn't even there, as if the hand I was holding didn't even belong to him. As if he was ashamed. As if he was embarrassed. Maybe he just had forgotten what a few moments before he seemed to want so desperately. It was impossible to know. Please, he would say, holding his hand out as far as it would go. As if he was afraid he was going to drown.

His mother died on St. Valentine's Day in her eighties, and Johnny in his sixties seemed utterly oblivious of it. Even when, as always, he was taken to her house for Sunday lunch and she wasn't there, he gave no sign of noticing. We wondered if he knew. Yes, Ralph said, he knew. And when he told him, Ralph said, tears had run down his big, solemn face.

But I wonder. I cannot picture it because I never saw him in tears. I cannot imagine anything hitting so close to whoever he was in the deepest part of himself. Maybe Ralph was just trying to keep his fictional personality alive.

What I picture instead is those little shapely, pursed lips and raised eyebrows as he sat there silent and unmoving while Ralph did his best to explain what had happened.

Soon after he died I wrote a poem about him which I read in the Jupiter Island cemetery behind the chapel where three of our small towheaded grandchildren—Dylan, Tristan, and Caroline—helped fit the box with his ashes in it down into the newly dug hole like a piece of one of the puzzles he had spent so many years struggling with.

> He held the giraffe
> so long in his delicate
> hand he forgot
> the giraffe-shaped hole
> forgot where he was
> who he was if he knew
> like a president signing
> a bill into law
> he placed it at last
> upside down first
> then straight where it went
> the place it belonged
> tightening his lips
> in disdain like the only
> man in a room
> full of children
> his window gave out
> on the waterway windsurfing
> boys girls all gold
> in bikinis a pelican
> perched on the dock

if anyone opened
the door his lament
rose at the end
to the shrill of Oedipus
blinded a cow
giving birth
they lowered him into
the pool in a harness
hoisted him into
a van in his chair
drove him anywhere miles

a nurse said he grasped
almost all that he heard
said once in the dark
he woke with his father's
name on his lips
some line from a song
sometimes he reached out his hand
to whoever was there
to strangers to touch them
please he said please

sometimes he turned
his slow head with a smile
that could break your heart
break the pane in the window
let in the water
the sky the pelican
robed like a prince
like a shining prince
like a shining.

Presidents I Have Known

The first president I ever saw was Franklin D. Roosevelt. It was in 1933 when he was about fifty, and I was about six. He was living in the White House, and I was living, also in Washington, at a residential hotel called the Dresden while my mother was looking around for a house she knew we couldn't afford in a neighborhood she considered suitable. One day she, my younger brother Jamie, and I found ourselves in the lobby of the Mayflower Hotel for some reason. To use the john? To come in out of the weather? I suppose it might even be that somebody had tipped my mother off, and she had brought Jamie and me along so we would have something to tell our grandchildren someday. Jamie never had any grandchildren, but I did, and I have told them.

There were a lot of people milling around under the high ceiling, a lot of gilded mirrors and polished mahogany and deep carpeting with bellboys in pillbox hats doing errands and men in morning coats standing behind the registration desk. Then suddenly everybody seemed to start murmuring at once. "He's coming! He's coming!" they were saying, and when I asked my mother who they were talking about, she said, "They're talking about the president. President Roosevelt is coming."

I can see us standing there waiting for him. Jamie and I are wearing short trousers with knee socks and sweaters that buttoned at the shoulder. Jamie's garters are showing because he rarely folded the tops of his socks down over them properly. He has on a navy blue cap with a button at the top. I am capless and my hair is in bangs. I am about two years older than Jamie and about a head taller. Our mother has a coat with a fur collar over one arm and is holding a purse. She is wearing a black beret with a diamond circle pinned to it. Her sleek blonde hair glints in the light of the chandelier. Like all the other women there, she has on lipstick and is wearing silk stockings and high heels.

She is in her mid-thirties and not happy about living at the Dresden. She wants a house of her own, preferably in Georgetown because that is where nice people live and it has brick sidewalks and pleasant little trees to give you shade in the summer. My father works at the *Washington Evening Star* because one of his Princeton classmates is a son of the family who owns it and wangled him a job driving around through the Virginia countryside checking to make sure the paper has been properly stuffed into the delivery tubes in front of people's houses. My mother says she is embarrassed to tell people what he does, but he says a lot of men he knows are standing in bread lines and he was lucky to get anything. Their marriage is not doing well. When they go out to parties, he usually has too much to drink, and my mother tells him he is weak and worthless. She says that in her wildest dreams as a girl she never thought she would end up like this. It was hard for me to imagine anybody who was a mother ever having been a girl and harder still to imagine those dreams. She looked so lovely and peaceful standing there with the chandelier light in her hair. I wondered what it was that had been so wild about them.

I don't know how much Jamie took in of her tirades. He was only about four years old at the time, a wiry, stalwart little figure with his garters showing. Sometimes, without any warning, he launched off into tirades of his own. We called them his "speeches." He would suddenly climb up on a big wooden chest we had in the dining room and start working himself into a frenzy. He would wave his arms around and jump up and down like Jiminy Cricket on his bandy little legs and, with his face turning red, would let fly with an impassioned diatribe that was all the more powerful because none of us could understand a word of it. My parents laughed, and I guess I laughed along with them, but it was less because I found it funny, I think, than that I didn't know what else to do. It confused me to see the smallest and weakest among us suddenly become the only one of us who dared give vent to what was going on. "The ship is going *down!*" Is that what he was saying? "You generation of vipers! Even now the axe is laid to the root of the tree!"

Who knows what he was saying, that fiery little homunculus. In his quieter moments he used to drag around the house with the small, sour-smelling pillow he slept with at night dangling from his curled fingers, his thumb in his mouth and one eye goggling out at us over it. Sometimes he refused to get up and dressed in the morning and spent most of the day in bed. He said it was because his clothes didn't hang right, but I think it was because bed was the only place he felt safe.

Even all these years later I can still remember the moment when the double doors of the elevator rumbled softly apart and there was Franklin D. Roosevelt framed in the wide opening. He was standing between two men, the taller of whom, my mother whispered, was one of his sons. Each of them had hold of him under one of his arms, and I could see that if they let go of him, he would crumple to the ground on legs as flimsy as the legs of the Sleepy Sam dolls in their seersucker pajamas that Jamie and I took to bed with us at night. He was the most important man in the Mayflower Hotel. He was the most important man in the world. But I could see with my own eyes that if he didn't have those two men to help, he would be helpless.

In addition to the Sleepy Sams, Jamie and I also had Raggedy Andys. When we first got them, we took heart-shaped Necco wafers left over from Valentine's Day and made slits in their chests so we could push them into their cottony insides. They were pink hearts with "I love you" printed on them, and once they were in place, somebody stitched the slits up again so they wouldn't fall out. I have sometimes wondered what becomes of the toys of our childhood. I suppose most of them just fall to pieces or get lost or are thrown out. But there must be at least a few of them that survive. Maybe one of the Raggedy Andys still exists in some obscure corner of the world—tucked way at the back of a drawer in a house miles away from Georgetown, or in a cardboard box full of junk in some stranger's attic, or for sale at an antique shop because, even when they're missing one eye, seventy-five-year-old Raggedy Andys are worth something. It is dressed in faded blue overalls and a threadbare red and white striped shirt. In its insides, unbeknownst to anybody, is the Necco heart. "I love you," it says.

I love the three of them standing there in the Mayflower lobby—the pretty, discontented young woman and the two small, excited boys. The father is not with them because he is probably off in the country somewhere checking those delivery tubes. He died only four years later, so I remember almost nothing about him—not even what he looked like, not even the sound of his voice. But the words on the heart are for him anyway.

I love him for his terrible luck in marrying the wrong girl at the wrong time and for all those nothing jobs he took because they were the only jobs he could find. I love him for that early November morning in Essex Fells, New Jersey, when, before the sun had risen, he walked down two flights of stairs to the garage, turned on the Chevy, and then sat down on the running board with his head in his hands to wait. I love him for the few lines he wrote in pencil to my mother thinking she would be the only one to see them.

The day President Roosevelt died, a few years after our paths crossed at the Mayflower, I was a Pfc. holding down a nothing job of my own in the message center of the Infantry Replacement Training Center at Fort McClellan, Alabama.

Every hour or so I was supposed to deliver whatever new messages there might be to all the top brass in the Headquarters Building, and as I made my rounds that day, I was the one who in office after office broke the news about the president. Nobody quite believed me, he'd been around so long. I didn't quite believe myself.

What I learned for the first time from that glimpse I had of him in the elevator is that even the mightiest among us can't stand on our own. Unless we have someone to hold us, our flimsy legs buckle. My father made his way down the two flights of stairs as quietly as he could, then sat on the running board and waited. When he was discovered an hour or so later that morning, he was crumpled over like Sleepy Sam.

It was in Paris in 1956 that I had my encounter with Harry Truman. My young bride and I were on our honeymoon, staying for a few days in the elegant house of her uncle George Perkins, who was the U.S. ambassador to NATO then. At meals there was always a little porcelain menu at each place written out in the curlicue script the French seem to use only when describing food, and you never knew who might be there at the table with you. One evening, I remember, it was Lawrence Norstadt, if I have the name right, an air force general who was NATO's commander in chief. There had been a lot of stories about UFOs in the papers recently, and I asked him if as a military man he had any reason to believe they really existed. Several pilots he trusted without reservation had told him they had actually seen them, he said, and that was good enough for him.

My wife's parents were staying with the Perkinses at the same time we were, and on another evening they told us they wanted us to have dinner with them at the great Tour d'Argent where people flocked from all over the world to try the celebrated pressed duck. Not long after we were seated, there was a little stir at the door as a group of eight people was ushered in with great ceremony and placed at a table next to ours. Of the three French couples, the men were all political figures who at the time were immediately recognizable and with them, the guests of honor, were former President Harry Truman and his wife, Bess. Whereas Roosevelt had needed two men to hold him up, Truman gave the impression that it would have taken both of them together to hold him down— a vigorous-looking man—on the short side—with a broad smile and an energetic way of talking. Bess looked, as she always tended to, as though she would rather have stayed home. Then two things happened.

The first was that from the way the president was sitting with his back half turned toward me, I found it possible not only to look through his thick-lensed glasses but, more wonderful still, to look through them at *Bess*. Just possibly nobody except the president had ever done that before, I thought. There she was—stout, dowdy, making the best of things as she tried to think of what to say next to their fancy hosts. With a Raggedy Andy heart inside him, the Bess he saw was of course not the Bess I saw, but the fact that we were both seeing her through the same glasses made it almost seem so. Even though he was unaware of it, I felt a kind of bond between us that my own heart was touched by.

The second thing was soon to follow. At some point during our meal the maître d'hôtel approached his distinguished guests begging a thousand pardons for the interruption and asking permission to show President Truman the spectacular view that was right there outside the window. At a signal, all the lights were turned off in the restaurant, and suddenly there it all was: the floodlit cathedral of Notre Dame where Joan of Arc was beatified, Napoleon crowned, and prayers offered for deliverance from the Black Death. The Seine like a river of stars. The glittering necklace of lights along the quai. The April moon.

All in a moment it was laid out before us for the sake of that one small man from Missouri with his double-breasted suit and wire-rimmed glasses and the woman beside him he referred to as the Boss.

It was the second time my heart was touched that evening in the Tour d'Argent.

∾

I had President Eisenhower's grandson, David, in several of my classes during the years I taught at Exeter. He was a pleasant, open-faced, intelligent boy who struck me as having successfully avoided the usual pitfalls of being related to somebody so famous. He didn't either seek out the limelight or hide away in the shadows but seemed genuinely unconcerned with his special status and went about his business much like everybody else. When Ike had his heart attack and was occasionally seen in his hospital window waving down at reporters, I remember remarking to him one day that his grandfather was a tough old bird, but apart from that I don't think his name was ever mentioned between us.

My mother-in-law was a great Eisenhower fan, as was reflected in a dream I had about her once. She was visibly pregnant, age eighty-two or whatever she was, and when I asked her who the father was, she hesitated for a moment and then said she *thought* it was General Eisenhower.

She seemed to enjoy the dream when I told her about it, but as a rule we avoided talking about him because our views were so different. He was so *spiritual*, she often said, by which she seemed to mean simply he had a nice smile and a friendly manner and looked well in his army uniform with all those ribbons pinned to it. As far as I was concerned, he not only spent far too much time on the golf course with people like Bob Hope and Bing Crosby but was also sorely lacking in moral courage. When Joe McCarthy accused Ike's old friend General George C. Marshall of being a Communist, Ike never spoke out in his defense, and during the civil rights crisis in the South he failed to take a firm stand against school segregation. When Governor Faubus of Arkansas threatened to prevent a black child from being allowed to enter the doors of the Little Rock high school, he ended up doing his presidential duty by calling out the National Guard, and the day was saved. But if only with his enormous prestige and great popularity he had gone down to Arkansas and personally led that child up the school stairs, he could have changed the course of history.

He didn't do that, but years later what he did do was agree to speak at the Exeter commencement the spring that David graduated. There was a small luncheon for him beforehand, and it was then that I got my first look at him, sat near him at the same table in fact, even shook his hand. He looked exactly as I'd seen him in countless pictures—that partly cherubic, partly goblinlike pink face and bald head—but what I was not prepared for was his smile. It was not a public relations smile, a vote-getting smile, a smile he'd worked up for the occasion. It was an utterly spontaneous smile. It was a smile that held nothing back and asked nothing back. It was so beautiful, it all but justified my mother-in-law's "spiritual." It lit up the room. And after all those years of bad-mouthing him and not voting for him, I knew that if the occasion arose I would follow him even into the jaws of death.

The Exeter principal must have spoken some word of welcome, and Ike must have made some kind of response, and as the school minister I must have been called on to say some kind of grace, but all of that I have long since forgotten. The smile, on the other hand, I have remembered ever since—the smile of a man at the absolute best he had it in him to be and somehow evoking the best of each of us who was there to behold it.

Commencement itself had a wonderfully nineteenth-century air about it. It was a gorgeous New Hampshire afternoon with bright sun and a cloudless sky and a platform draped in red, white, and blue bunting set up on the lawn in front of the Academy Building. There were row upon row of folding chairs filling up with parents and assorted well-wishers, some of them fanning themselves with their tasseled programs. Mamie was there in the front row, of course, with her pretty hat and bangs. The school band was there in their red blazers and ice-cream-white slacks. The faculty was lining up to come marching in arrayed in all their academic finery with the black-gowned seniors in their mortarboards to follow behind them.

As the one who was to give the invocation I was among the handful who were to sit up on the platform, and for a few moments, waiting for the show to start, Ike and I stood together side by side in the shade of one of the tall elms. From somewhere a stray dog appeared, wandering up and down the aisle with his tail in the air and his nose to the ground as he snuffed at people's feet and occasionally lifted his leg if he found a spot that especially appealed to him. I said to Ike I thought I had never attended a commencement where a dog like him hadn't turned up somewhere along the line—it seemed to be part of the tradition—and he said he agreed. There were just the two of us side by side there awaiting our cue, and for as long as the moment lasted we were as easy together as old friends.

He remembered one West Point commencement in particular, he said. The inevitable dog had shown up but instead of rambling around aimlessly like this one had made his way up the stairs to the platform before anyone could stop him. The cadets were filing by one by one and the dog took his place among them. When whoever it was that was handing out the diplomas saw him approach, Ike told me, he halted the proceedings. "I'm sorry," he said, "but we have to draw the line somewhere."

The old president who was there to see his only grandson move one step closer to striking out into the cold world. The young school minister who, four years after seeing President Roosevelt at the Mayflower Hotel, ran into the cold world head-on one November morning at sunrise and who had looked out at that same world for a few moments through President Truman's glasses. We had our little laugh together, President Eisenhower and I, and for the last time I got to see that smile that made me almost believe that maybe everything would turn out all right in the end even so.

Wunderjahr

In the summer of 1950, at the age of twenty-four, I set sail for Europe on a small British freighter named the *Rialto*. My first novel, *A Long Day's Dying*, had gotten my name in the papers all over the place as well as in every magazine you can think of. Leonard Bernstein wanted me to collaborate with him on an opera libretto, and Carl Van Vechten with his snaggle teeth leered down at me through the blinding floods like a Halloween pumpkin as he photographed me for posterity. On the strength of all this I decided to take a year off from teaching English at my old school, Lawrenceville, and to spend it in Europe writing novel number two. The *Rialto*, not much bigger than a rich man's yacht, left from Hoboken, and my mother and Naya, my eighty-three-year-old grandmother, came to see me off, Naya skittering up the steeply inclined gangplank as nimble as an old gray squirrel. There were only about a dozen passengers all told, most of them working-class people from Hull, where we were scheduled to land, and one of them was a woman of such enormous girth that Naya said she would lay odds that I wouldn't get to see her for nothing once we reached the other side.

A Lawrenceville colleague and Princeton classmate named Ned Hughes, who had plans to spend the summer studying at Oxford, was on the *Rialto* too, and we took our meals at the same table as an old gentleman named Shackleton, who claimed to be related to the Antarctic explorer and every morning at breakfast brought us up to date, with hair-raising detail, on the current state of his digestion. Brown Windsor soup, mutton, and overcooked vegetable marrow were the staples of our diet together with a dessert called Vermicelli pudding, which turned out to be cold spaghetti covered with treacle. Since we had nothing much else to do on the ten-day voyage, Ned and I helped pass the time by playing endless games of checkers. To my horror I won every single one of them no matter how hard I tried not to, and though he was such a passive, good-natured sort of person that it didn't seem to bother him at all, it left me hardly able to face myself in the mirror.

The great joy and drama of the voyage turned out to be the ocean itself. As a child I had made the trip to Bermuda a number of times during the few years we lived there on the eve of the Second World War, but from the deck of one of the great top-heavy Cunarders—the *Monarch* and *Queen of Bermuda*—even when the waves were at their most mountainous they seemed unreal and remote from the dizzying height of the deck where we stood to watch them. But on the chunky little *Rialto* as she made her dogged way eastward, they were a continuously imposing presence. We did not so much cut our way through them as we slid slowly up their glassy, wrinkled flanks scattered with white foam like heather until we could see nothing but sky ahead and then plunged into the abyss at breathtaking speed with tons of water thundering down behind us. Even on calm days the swells were so great that there were times when the horizon completely disappeared, and you couldn't walk without having to take little mincing steps forward to keep from falling on your face as the deck gave way beneath you or, as it rose into the sky, bending almost double to climb it. I remember in particular one brilliantly sunny day toward the end of our voyage. All around us the sea was nothing but whitecaps, and as the wind whipped off their spray, the sun turned it every color of the spectrum so that we were surrounded by an endless meadow of rainbows.

Another moment I have always remembered was walking out on deck one night after supper and finding a young red-haired officer peering into the dark through binoculars. He told me he was scanning the horizon for signs of other ships, and the way to do that, he explained, was to look not at the horizon but just above it. He said you could see better that way than by looking straight on, and I have found it to be an invaluable truth in many ways. Listen not just to the words being spoken but to the silences between the words, and watch not just the drama unfolding on the stage but the faces all around you watching it unfold. Years later when preaching a sermon about Noah, it was less the great flood that I tried to describe than the calloused palm of Noah's hand as he reached out to take the returning dove, less the resurrection itself than the moment, a day or so afterward, when Jesus stood on the beach cooking fish on a charcoal fire and called out to the disciples in their boat, "Come and have breakfast."

Because of some sort of strike, the *Rialto* was unable to land at Hull as scheduled—much to the disgruntlement of all the Hull citizens, including the fat lady I was going to have to pay to see once we arrived—and steamed up the Thames to land in London instead. It was there at the Tilbury docks that in 1588 Queen Elizabeth I (as if there could ever be another) reviewed her troops on the eve of the Armada. The Earl of Leicester was mounted on her left with his fiery-haired stepson, the young Earl of Essex, on her right, and between them, on a white horse with dappled gray hindquarters, the Queen herself wearing a silver corselet over her white velvet dress and gripping a truncheon in her hand as she shrilled out to the soldiers, "I know I have but the body of a weak and feeble woman, but I have the heart and stomach of a king, and of a King of England too."

A first cousin of my father's, Peggy Zinsser, had married Lewis Douglas, who was then our ambassador to England, and knowing that I would be passing through London she invited me to come stay with them until I decided where I wanted to settle down in France. So while poor Ned Hughes, fresh from his humiliation at the checkerboard, slunk off to find a hotel he could afford, I took a cab to the ambassadorial residence at 13 Prince's Gate, just across from where Kensington Gardens and Hyde Park meet. There was a pair of bobbies standing watch outside, and the door was opened by Mr. Epps, the quintessential head butler, who was reported to have been so corrupted by the Douglas sons' Americanisms that when a visitor asked one day if he could see Mr. Douglas, his reply was, "I'm sorry, sir, but His Excellency is in the sack."

Lew Douglas, Franklin D. Roosevelt's budget director in the 1930s, was a soft-spoken man of great kindness and courtesy who wore a black patch over one eye as the result of getting a hook caught in it while fly-fishing with friends in Scotland, and his wife was a lively, intelligent woman with flashing dark eyes and a facial tic that my mother found so attractive that when they first knew each other in Washington she said she used to stand in front of the mirror trying to emulate it. The Douglases and I were the only ones at dinner that first evening, and when at some point Mr. Epps came in to announce, "Your Excellency, Mr. Churchill is on the phone," I felt I had my finger on the pulse of history.

When dinner was over, they suggested I might like to take a stroll through Kensington Gardens just across the street and gave me a key of my own to let myself back in with. I remember still the enchantment of it—the haloes of the street lamps in the hazy dusk, the shallow Serpentine reflecting the moon, the statue of Peter Pan with his pipe at his lips, but most of all just the excitement of being in England at last which I had dreamed of since early childhood, having come to know it first through E. Nesbit, and Dr. Doolittle, and Eleanor and Herbert Farjeon's *Kings and Queens,* which gave me a taste for English history that has stayed with me ever since. I was so enthralled by actually being there that I ended up spending the better part of a month with the inexhaustibly hospitable Douglases before moving on to France. I was assigned a valet named Robert, who brought me my breakfast on a tray every morning together with a crisp new copy of the *Times,* whose front page in those days was always the court circular no matter how earthshaking the news inside, and who saw to it that my shoes were kept polished, my laundry done, and my clothes hung neatly cleaned and pressed in the closet.

You never knew who you might run into downstairs—Sir Malcolm Sargent, Danny Kaye, Isaiah Berlin among others were frequent visitors—and one day, just as I was about to go out, the Douglases' daughter Sharman, my second cousin, collared me in the black-and-white-tiled hall and said I must come meet her friend Princess Margaret, who was there for cocktails. I was not prepared for how tiny she was—hardly as high as my shoulder with her bright eyes glistening and the loveliest rose petal complexion I have ever seen. I should address her as Ma'am, Sharmy whispered on our way into the drawing room, but it was only later that she told me you were always supposed to let royalty be the ones to introduce the subject of conversation, whereas I in my ignorance had babbled on about some movie I had just seen.

I also met my English publishers, Chatto and Windus, for the first time. They were located in a tall mid-Victorian building on King William IV Street not far from St. Martin-in-the-Fields. There was a photograph of Mark Twain hanging on the battleship-gray walls of the shabby waiting room near T. S. Eliot's signed contract for the first publication of *The Waste Land,* and the bare white lobby was cluttered with bicycles, brown paper packages waiting to be picked up by visored messengers on motorbikes, and a small glass cubicle containing an ancient switchboard. A cast-iron staircase led to the upper floors where the offices were, and while climbing it one day I was introduced in the shadows to a sallow, spidery figure who turned out to be Leonard Woolf.

There was also an old elevator with a tightly sprung wooden door that you had to hold open with your elbows while struggling with the metal grille inside. My editor, Norah Smallwood, told me she had gotten stuck in it one day along with her handsome, urbane colleague Ian Parsons and the venerable Harold Raymond, the firm's chairman. She said there was just enough space at the bottom of the cab to see to the ground floor if you got down on your hands and knees, and spotting a janitor walking by, one of them shouted at him through the opening. The janitor disappeared for a while, she said, and then returned with a hand-lettered sign reading "Out of Order" which he hung on the door before disappearing, as far as they knew, for the rest of the day.

Norah Smallwood and I became great friends for the next twenty years or so, and the last time we met—I made the long trip from Vermont down to New York and back again the same day just to have lunch with her—she was so crippled with arthritis that she had to walk with a cane. But in 1950 when we first knew each other she looked much as I imagined the first Queen Elizabeth had when she delivered herself of those memorable words at Tilbury. She had a keen, triangular face with penetrating blue eyes, curling reddish hair, and a wonderfully deep, resounding laugh. Her tyranny at Chatto's was legendary. She battled with, brutalized, banished anybody who got in her way so that the dusty corridors on William IV Street often echoed with the sound of hapless underlings sobbing into their handkerchiefs or slamming doors in helpless frustration over their last terrible encounter.

But with me, because I was one of her authors and because from the beginning she had taken a shine to me, she was unfailingly charming and warm and enormous fun to be with. She was always enthusiastic about my books even though their English sales were consistently disappointing and was as delighted as I was when *The Return of Ansel Gibbs* was reissued as a Penguin. On her first trip to New York I gave a cocktail party for her with as many literary lights as I could assemble, including Jean Stafford, William Inge, Louis Auchincloss, and little Oscar Williams with the usual brown paper bag full of his anthologies which he handed out to anyone who looked interested; and when my new bride and I went to London on our honeymoon in 1956, she got us reservations at the old Cavendish Hotel on

Jermyn Street where we were given a suite of moth-eaten elegance by its little manager, Edie, who was Norah's friend as well as, some said, the daughter of Rosa Lewis, the hotel's former owner, by Edward VII. As the ambassador's daughter and the good friend of Princess Margaret as well as of her older sister, Elizabeth, Sharman Douglas, Sharmy—named for our common great-grandfather, H. B. Scharmann—was the toast of the town. Pert and blonde with sleepy eyes and a spontaneous, throaty laugh, she could go nowhere without being recognized. Sunny Blandford, later to become the Duke of Marlborough, was one of her suitors and Peter Lawford, the actor, another, and she knew and was known by virtually everybody. She took me to the Palladium with her one evening to hear a concert by her friend Frank Sinatra, whom she introduced me to in his dressing room, and when the two of us left the theater through the stage door, the waiting crowd, thinking I must be Peter Lawford or some other immortal, crowded around with their cameras and autograph books giving me a taste of what it must be like to be a *Celebrity*.

My second taste came when Lew Douglas invited me to go with him to Edinburgh where he was to be awarded the Freedom of the City, and we flew up together in a small government plane—the first time I had ever flown anywhere. At a reception in his honor soon after we arrived, one of the many notables in attendance was the dashing young movie star Douglas Fairbanks Jr., and somehow or other it got into the mind of an ancient former Lord Provost named Sir John Falconer that I was he. Clearly delighted to be associated with anybody so glamorous, he took me by the arm and led me around the room introducing me to anybody he could lay his hands on with remarks like "Mary Pickford's boy, you know" and "a chip off the old block" while I stood helplessly by not wanting to humiliate the old gentleman by pointing out his mistake, which the people he introduced me to were as aware of as I so that for all I knew they believed the imposture was of my own contriving.

Instead of flying back to London we went by car, stopping for the weekend with the Douglases' friends the Duke and

Duchess of Buccleuch—Walter and Molly—at Drumlanrig Castle, their seat at Dumfries in the border country. The duchess I had already been captivated by in Edinburgh, a handsome, vivid woman of great charm and wit who I was told was famous for having had a string of lovers over the years and who, Peggy Douglas confided in me later, she thought had her eye a little on me.

What the duchess told me herself at some event we attended together was that she was descended directly from both Mary Queen of Scots and Pocahontas, adding to whoever happened to be nearby that the reason she mentioned it was that she knew Americans were impressed by that sort of thing, as indeed I was. Her husband, the duke, was what P. G. Wodehouse would have called "a pink chap" with almost invisibly blond eyebrows and eyelashes, and it was he who had made the formal presentation at the Freedom of City ceremony. The duchess—whom I never knew what to call since only the servants used "Your Grace" and just plain "Duchess" made her sound like something out of *Alice in Wonderland*—sent me later a photograph she had taken of the Douglases and me sitting on the parapet of the castle, Lew grinning into the sunlight with his black eyepatch in place and the Buccleuch emblem—a winged heart surmounted by a coronet—carved here and there into the pinkish gray stone the eighteenth-century castle was made of.

It was Lady Caroline Scott, one of the Buccleuchs' daughters, who gave me a tour of some of the castle's treasures including letters from various people who had stayed there over the years like Sir Walter Scott, Alexander Pope, and Dr. Johnson, and a stunning collection of sixteenth- and seventeenth-century miniatures by Nicholas Hilliard. She also told me about the legend of the Black Box, discovered by some earlier duke, which was supposed to have contained the wedding certificate of Charles II and his mistress Lucy Walter proving that their son, the Duke of Monmouth, from whom the Buccleuchs traced their line and title, was the legitimate heir to the throne. There were two theories about what had become of the document, she said. One of them was that the duke who discovered it pronounced that no loyal Englishman should keep such a bomb-shell in his possession and promptly set it on fire. The other was that he took it to Queen Victoria, who after one horrified glance set it on fire herself. If it were ever rediscovered, I asked Caroline, a pretty, slightly condescending young woman about my age, what would that make her father, and I can still remember the solemn resonance of her reply. "The King," she said.

The next day there was a grouse-shooting expedition up into the moors, and I was asked to drive the car that took, among others, Caroline's older sister Elizabeth, the enormously pregnant young Duchess of Northumberland. Our road was a precipitous dirt track which I followed full of trepidation at the thought that if I went over the edge, coronets would topple and ancient titles go begging. At one of the gates we had to pause at on our way, a tenant farmer who came out to open it presented the duchess with the most decayed and derelict-looking tweed gillies hat I have ever seen. It must have gotten buried under the snow the previous winter, he said, doffing his cap, but recognizing it as belonging to her grace, he thought she might like to have it back again, and if it had been a diamond tiara or proof of her husband's right to the throne, she couldn't have seemed more grateful and pleased. Once we arrived at our destination in the moors where the gillies flushed the birds, everybody but me had at them in a blaze of gunfire that left the ground littered with their bodies, one of which, near me, was thrashing about not entirely dead. Would I mind wringing its neck, the descendant of Charles II not to mention of Pocahontas and Mary Queen of Scots asked, and the best I could do was pretend I hadn't heard her. But she nonetheless took my hand in hers when it came time to head for home and allowed me to help her into the car.

But the most memorable part of my visit took place the next morning. I had a single room on the ground floor of the castle, and when I woke up, it was filled with the thin gray light that comes just before dawn. There was a large wing chair catty-cornered to my bed, and when I rolled over in that direction I found that it was occupied by a faceless white presence of such great size that if it had stood up, it would have had to bow its head to avoid hitting the ceiling. I had the sense that it had been there silent and unmoving for hours, maybe for centuries, and I was so startled that I took a second look to make sure I wasn't dreaming only to find that it was still hugely and unmistakably there. Instead of saying something to it such as asking it who it was or what it wanted, I pulled the bedclothes over my head and lay there sweating with terror that it would come over and pull them off. It was unlike anything I had ever felt before—not a fear that something terrible would happen but a fear simply of being there in that unearthly presence—a fear as faceless and overwhelming as the presence itself. I don't know how long I lay there before I finally heard the blessedly everyday sound of a vacuum cleaner in some other part of the castle, which gave me courage to risk taking one peek from under the bedclothes. What I found was that the chair was empty.

Two things. First, on undressing the night before, I had laid my white shirt over the back of the chair, not spreading it out but just letting it lie, a narrow swath of white cloth, where it happened to fall. Second, behind the chair there was a dressing table with a framed mirror that was tilted slightly backward so that it reflected the white ceiling. I tried to convince myself that what I had seen was no more than the product of those two things, but I couldn't manage it. Nothing so simple could explain not only what I had seen but also what had made my blood run cold as never before or since in my life. Besides that, I had had not just one quick look at it but a second, slower one to make sure, and for years afterward when I let my mind stray back, the indescribable uncanniness of whatever unearthly thing it may have been was still so fresh that I felt my original terror all over again. Not wanting to make the Buccleuchs feel guilty for having put me through such an ordeal I made no mention of it at breakfast, but when I told my cousin Sharmy about it later, she merely laughed and said that everybody knew Drumlanrig was swarming with ghosts.

About two months later, I decided it was time to get on with my life, and taking along Lew Douglas's bike, which he thought might come in handy when I set off to search the countryside for a place to write, I finally took a channel steamer to France, where Paris, when I finally got there, proved to be as much a disappointment as London had been a delight. Peggy Douglas had recommended the Hotel Westminster on the Rue de la Paix where the only room I could afford was small and grim, and I spent hours there under the eaves reading Stendhal in French in between bouts of diarrhea. Several Smith girls I had known from college days were staying at Reed Hall, and I invited one of them to go with me to call on Alice B. Toklas, whom Carl Van Vechten had written to be nice to me. She turned out to be a very small woman with dark bangs and a moustache, and shared her apartment, which was hung with paintings by former friends of hers and Gertrude's, with the last of the white French poodles they named Basket. She served us tea with little flat, heart-shaped pastries called *coeurs de France*, and it wasn't until after her death that I learned from Mary McCarthy that she had taken to spending her winters mostly in bed because she couldn't afford adequate heating.

The other Smith girl I looked up was one I had been in love with as a senior at Princeton. In a moment of madness on my twenty-first birthday at the St. Regis roof, I had asked her to marry me, and if she hadn't had the good sense to say no, I shudder to think what would have become of us. By this time, three years later, I wasn't in love with her anymore but tried my best to be again and with part of my heart yearned to be above all things as she showed me around Paris in her bare-backed cotton dresses and ballet slippers speaking what after a year or so of living there had become her almost flawless French. One day we took the train out to Versailles and spent hours wandering through the acres of flower beds, the stately *allées*, the groves of tall, sad trees and grottoes deep in shadow where water trickled down out of the moss-covered rock walls. We ate our bread and cheese by the great *Bassin d'Apollon* where the god with a face modeled after *le Roi Soleil*'s rose out of the spangled water in a chariot surrounded by conch-blowing tritons and crowned with laurels, holding in one hand the reins of his four rearing chargers with their flared nostrils and flailing hooves. Wherever the water was still and unmoving we looked deep into such fathoms of sky that there was almost a fear of falling down, down into the dizzying altitude of it.

It was the most haunted place I had ever seen. There were ghosts everywhere—the print of a silken slipper in the wet grass, the flicker of a powdered wig among the rose trees, the echo of women's laughter—and I found my eyes full of tears as we walked. They were tears at all that vanished life and beauty, of course, but they were tears also at knowing that the girl at my side hadn't even noticed them and wouldn't have been likely to understand what on earth had caused them if she had. Our day was as over and done with as the days of Versailles's glory.

It was only a week or two later that my idea of staying in France and coming to love it as Naya did seemed more than I could manage. I missed the sound of my own language and after a day or two of speaking only French felt cross-eyed with exhaustion. I didn't know where or how to start looking for a place in the country, and if I ever found one, didn't know how I would ever manage to start a new life surrounded by strangers. I missed the feeling that from the beginning I had had in England that in some sense I had come home, the feeling I had always had, in Westminster Abbey especially, that all the dead past enshrined there was far from dead in me. Elizabeth Tudor and Bloody Mary in their single tomb—"Consorts both in throne and grave, here rest we two sisters in the hope of one resurrection"; "O Rare Ben Jonson" buried standing up beneath his bit of paving stone because that was all the space his friends could afford; Charles Dickens, Saint Edward the Confessor, Gentleman Johnny Burgoyne—they were my family, and we belonged together. So back across the channel I went, and though I felt some guilt at having given up France so easily, I knew I was heading in the right direction and hoped Naya would understand.

❧

After a relatively brief stay this time at Prince's Gate, where I returned the ambassadorial bicycle which I had used only once in a hair-raising circuit of the Étoile, I found my way, thanks to Peggy Douglas and the English-Speaking Union, to a village only a few miles from Oxford called Great Milton (slightly smaller than nearby Little Milton) where I rented a room in an Elizabethan manor run as a guest house by a family named Bell. I was the only American in the place, and the others all British and elderly. Mr. Charles Bickmore is the one I remember most vividly, a retired civil servant who had spent years in the foreign service. Tall, bony, with pinched nostrils, rosy cheeks, and thinning gray hair, he was a shy, fastidious old bachelor given to fits of wild intolerance and eccentricity. We all took our meals together at a common table waited on by an effeminate young man from the neighborhood named Colin, and one day when a plump female guest turned up for dinner wearing slacks, Mr. Bickmore rose from his chair, crawled under the table, and for several unforgettable minutes howled there like a dog at the moon.

He had spent years as a consul of some sort in Ceylon, and at tea one afternoon started inveighing against the incompetence of the native officials he had been obliged to work with. He cited as an example the way they invariably bungled the hangings that, as representative of the Crown, he was obliged to witness. The kind of rope they used, the knot, the hood, the height of the drop, all of it was so mismanaged that he said he finally had to step in and with his own hands show them how to do it properly—all of this as he spread his bread with strawberry jam, his eyes lowered to avoid having to catch any of ours.

For one reason or another I was the only one he got along with. The Bells said it was simply because he knew I was some sort of connection of the American ambassador's, and maybe they were right, but we seemed to enjoy each other's company in any case, and when I returned to England some six years later with my new young bride, he invited us to have tea with him wherever it was he had moved to after Great Milton and later took us to see the Leander club boathouse on the Thames where he pointed out a framed photograph of his young self and his fellow oarsmen standing by their eight-man shell as Oxford undergraduates.

My second-floor bedroom faced out on the village church that rang the changes every Sunday with first one bell and then another shifting its place in the sequence after every peal as I lay in bed trying to see if I could keep track of it. I did my writing there in the mornings, my notebook in my lap, and in the afternoons usually took the green double-decker bus that careened its top-heavy way along the narrow country roads into Oxford. Browsing once through Blackwell's, whose vast stock of books of every sort not only dazzled the eye but delighted the nose as you cracked open each stiff new volume to that faint, dry whiff of the arcane and scholarly that is to be found nowhere else, I ran into a Princeton philosophy professor named Jim Smith, whom I had never met before but knew by reputation as he knew me. He was on a one-year teaching exchange at Christ Church, and after we became friends I often had dinner with him there at high table beneath the fifty-foot ceiling of that cavernous medieval hall under the splenetic gaze of Holbein's Henry VIII, who himself had banqueted there. After dinner, the custom was to withdraw to some sanctum of the dons where a bottle of port was passed around from one of us to another with ritual solemnity—if it became empty on your turn you had to do something so complicated I no longer remember it—followed by snuff, which Smith showed me how to take without ever, under any circumstances, blundering into a sneeze. C. S. Lewis, whom Smith slightly knew, dined there occasionally too, but to my great regret I never made any effort to meet him or to hear him lecture because at that point in my life I knew nothing about him except, dimly, his name.

Smith had a little café au lait–colored Hillman Minx in which we made a tour of the great southern cathedrals including my favorite, Wells, so filled with light and air with its fantastically inverted arches and slender columns fanning out like feather dusters into the shadowy vaulting. Our longest trip

took us as far as the resort town of Llandudno at the northern-
most tip of Wales where we stayed at a hotel so nearly deserted
at that off-season that we were the only customers in its American Bar, where with great pride the bartender insisted on making us what as Americans he said we would be sure to recognize
as a classical martini which, after being spun around in a blender
with a generous amount of grenadine syrup and a maraschino
cherry on top, turned out as frothy and pink as a strawberry ice
cream soda.

In November, with the Bells having thriftily not yet turned
on the central heating, the Manor got so frigid that after dinner the guests lined up their chairs in order of seniority in front
of the coal fire, and my room was so frigid in the mornings that
I dropped a fortune into my small shilling stove which nearly
singed my trousers from the knees down but left my hands so
stiff with cold that I ended up getting back into bed to write.
The trouble with that was that more often than not I fell asleep
and got virtually nothing accomplished.

My oldest friend, Jimmy, from Lawrenceville days—the
poet James Merrill as he later became—was spending the winter on the island of Mallorca with his friend Claude Fredericks,
whom he had first met at the cocktail party Knopf gave to hail
the publication of *A Long Day's Dying*, and when he wrote asking if I would like to join them for a week or two, I leaped at
the chance. On the same day that George Bernard Shaw
died—I remember the papers were all full of it—I crossed the
Channel once again and after a night train to Marseilles took a
small steamer to Palma where Jimmy and Claude were waiting
for me on the dock looking like the Rover Boys in their match-
ing lederhosen.

The Hotel Maricel, where they were staying and had
booked me a room, was only a short tram ride from Palma. It
was a building of surpassing elegance—all marble floors, cedar
walls, and glittering chandeliers—and like everything else on
the island during those years right after the war was so unbe-
lievably cheap that I remember paying a barber ten cents to
come all the way out from the city to give me a haircut and

having a tweed jacket made to order for something like ten dollars. Having been completed only a month or so earlier, the Maricel was about two-thirds empty and run by a middle-aged Scandinavian woman of great charm and efficiency named Miss Petersen, who managed the desk and could have been the headmistress of a fashionable girls' school, and Mr. Miro, who seemed to run everything else, a kind and obliging Spaniard with patent-leather hair whom I tried unsuccessfully to get a job teaching Spanish and French at Lawrenceville because his dream was somehow to get to America.

My room, like the one Jimmy and Claude shared, was spacious and airy, the French windows hung with floor-length muslin curtains that furled and unfurled in the breeze. It had its own balcony overlooking the Mediterranean where every morning a dark-eyed little maid straight out of *Le Nozze di Figaro* served me my breakfast which always included a flat, circular pastry called an *ensemada*. Sweetened with honey and big around as a dinner plate, *ensemadas* were so rich with butter that they left a film of it on your lips and soaked through the round pasteboard containers I saw people carrying them in on their way back from market.

Like me Jimmy and Claude were both writing—Jimmy on his poems and Claude on the journal he started keeping at the age of eleven or so which by now fills so many typed volumes of single-spaced onion-skin pages that it may well be the longest book in the history of mankind. And of course we traveled around to see the sights too including the cheerless, dank villa where Chopin and Georges Sand lived for a while, and the cathedral in Palma where we heard an orchestra play (why on earth have I remembered it all these years?) the overture to Rossini's *The Thieving Magpie*, and orchards of silvery gray olive trees, some as much a thousand years old, and stunted fig trees all twisted and muscular like wrestling dwarves. During the war, gasoline became so scarce that many of the cars were converted to run on olive pits, which spewed out oily black fumes from the trunk-sized burners in back as they puttered their way through the blossoming almond trees, the wheat fields, and orange groves. At the end of my two-week visit I left for Barcelona on a Toonerville trolley of a ship that gave the impression of being made of wicker as it creaked and shuddered all night in a high sea with cabin doors slamming open and shut and the sound of passengers retching operatically as it came through the thin walls between us.

I met Jim Smith in Paris where, with the Korean War heating up, the American consul told me that, since I'd never thought to inform my draft board that I was leaving the country, I'd better go home and check in with them. So I spent the ten days or so left motoring around with Smith in his little Hillman again. We saw Viollet-le-Duc's shamelessly restored Vézelay, the *jeu de son et lumière* at François Premier's Chambord with the horns of his huntsmen and the baying of his hounds echoing through the dark forest, Diane de Poitier's Chenonçeaux with its long gallery spanning the river Cher and the furniture in the widowed queen's bedroom all in black embroidered with silver tears. Through some friends we ran into who knew the woman who was Bernard Berenson's long-time secretary and companion, we were invited with them to the Villa Itati in San Gimignano outside of Florence, where, after a tour of his treasures, the great man himself was wheeled in to meet us. A dapper, autocratic little figure with a goatee, he asked each of us in turn to tell him our names and what it was that we did. Smith, when it came to him, said that he was a philosopher, and when B.B. replied, "What is your philosophy?" mumbled something to the effect that it would be impossible to answer in one sentence. "Any question that can be asked in one sentence can be answered in one sentence," the great man shot back, and without the blink of an eye passed on to whichever one of us came next.

We were in Rome on Christmas Eve and went to St. Peter's to hear Pius XII conduct mass. Because 1950 was Holy Year, the place was teeming with pilgrims from all over Europe, many of whom, like us, got there hours ahead of time. Some had even brought food to sustain them till the show got started, and every once in a while singing would break out like brushfire, "Adeste Fidelis" and "Heilige Nacht" frequently recurring because everybody seemed to know the Latin words to one and the German words to the other as we milled around, thousands of us, trying to get as close as we could to the papal altar with its huge baldachino of gilded bronze and the aisle kept clear with velvet ropes for the pope eventually to come down.

After several hours, there was a sudden hush and way off in the flickering distance I could see the Swiss Guard entering with the papal throne on poles on their shoulders and everybody shouting "*Viva il Papa! Viva il Papa!*" like children at a parade as the procession made its slow way across acres of mosaic. In all that renaissance of splendor with the Swiss Guard in the scarlet and gold uniforms that Michelangelo had designed for them, Pius himself was vested in plainest white with only a white silk skullcap on the back of his head. I can still see his face, lean and ascetic with a high-bridged nose and the lenses of his glasses so thick they made his eyes larger than life. Leaning slightly forward, he was peering into every face he could see including mine with extraordinary intensity as though searching for someone he had never yet found but would spend the rest of his life looking for. Was it this one? Was it that one? It was a moment of great power for me, and I felt certain that the one he was looking for was Christ.

In Pompeii we had a guide with a limp who for a price unlocked the shutters covering all the X-rated graffiti. In Ostia Antica we accidentally scuffed away some sand covering a terrace to reveal a patch of mosaic tiling which with increasing excitement we continued to clear thinking we were making archaeological history until a uniformed guard appeared from nowhere to tell us the sand was there to protect the mosaic from freezing temperatures and please to put it all back again.

We drove through the Simplon Tunnel out of Italy, all hot sun and red wine and pasta, into snow so deep we had to put chains on the tires before heading off into Switzerland, all milk and cheese and fresh-baked bread, as fresh and clean as laundry. In Geneva we found our way to the house of Naya's handsome blonde cousin Hélène Boissonas who looked a lot like my mother, and was horrified to be caught with her hair tied up in a scarf as she did the vacuuming. We also saw the house of Naya's Tante Élise Golay which stood in the shadow of Calvin's cathedral near a huge cherry tree which years earlier Tante Élise had rigged up with a bell she could ring by pulling a string from her garden to frighten the birds away.

It was sometime in early 1951 that I finally sailed back to New York on the old *De Grasse* after little more than half of what I had intended to be a full year of writing my book. Another of the Reed Hall Smith girls happened to be aboard, and I still have a pen-and-ink sketch she did of an old dowager whose deck chair was near ours all bundled up in a steamer rug with a newspaper held high in her spidery, black-gloved hands as she peered at it through a lorgnette.

The Seasons' Difference was the title I gave the book which I finally finished a few months later in my grandmother Buechner's New York apartment at 119 East Eighty-fourth Street. It was the most unsuccessful book I have ever written and deservedly so. I gave it an overtly Christian theme before I had any clear idea what Christianity was all about. The characters were all drawn from people I knew, including Jimmy Merrill and me as schoolboys, so that from time to time they act and sound a little like real people, but the story never comes together and, most importantly, I had not yet found either my own true voice as a writer or my own true subject. All the reviewers who had extolled *A Long Day's Dying* for the decadence and mandarin chic they found in it were appalled by my unprecedented turn to religion and almost universally panned it.

If that second novel had been as topical and racy as my four Bebb books, say, who knows how differently my career would have turned out. I might have become as much of a celebrity as acquaintances like Truman Capote, Norman Mailer, and Gore Vidal. Even Hollywood might have come knocking on my door. But partly because I was too absorbed in my teaching at Lawrenceville to have time for much else and partly because for one reason or another fame for the sake of fame never seems to have attracted me, I went my own way as a writer, alternately depressed or elated by the reviewers but never very seriously influenced by them.

Wandering and wondering never got into my blood as it did into Jimmy's. He ended up more or less leaving behind the world we had become friends in as boys and became the "different person" he describes in his memoirs. I on the other hand made what, literarily speaking, was the fatal career move of being ordained a Presbyterian minister, of all things, with the result that the literary establishment by and large dropped me like a hot Presbyterian potato. By staying at home both literally and figuratively I found my treasure not in the wide world as Jimmy did but in the humdrum unfolding of my own quite unextraordinary life with a wife and three children in southern Vermont.

And all in all I wouldn't have had it otherwise.

Fathers and Teachers

The first funeral I ever conducted was of a French teacher I had at Lawrenceville named George Rice Woods. His was also the first class I ever attended there one gray morning in the fall of 1940 as a homesick fourteen-year-old with hair parted in the middle and pimples. He was a dapper, fluttery little bachelor known to the boys as Boom Boom after a clown in one of the French stories he assigned us who beat a big bass drum like Caruso in *Pagliacci*. To make up for his diminutive stature he wore a pearl-gray fedora with an unusually high crown and fired his little feet like missiles at the floor when he walked so that windows rattled at his approach. "*Bonne chance!*" was what he wrote in my senior yearbook in a bold, dashing hand, and he came down so hard on the exclamation points that you can still see where the ink spattered.

Some five years after graduating from Lawrenceville I returned to teach English there, and the apartment I was assigned to was in Stone Cottage where Boom Boom also had his. I remember his living room particularly. There were bits of colored glass glittering in all the windows, pictures and posters on all the walls, and every available surface crowded with *objets*

and memorabilia of one kind or another mostly from France—
miniature books, china animals, restaurant ashtrays, souvenir
spoons—each with a story associated with it which he would
tell you at the drop of a hat. There were also a number of
framed photographs of students who had been his special
pets—good-looking boys in jackets and ties with their hair
slicked back.

When he retired from Lawrenceville, he moved to Exeter,
New Hampshire, where he shared a house with an elderly widowed cousin, Maybelle Favor, both of whose names were pronounced with the accent on the last syllable so that she
sounded like a burlesque queen. I dropped in on him every
once in a while—I was teaching at Phillips Exeter by then—
and to keep the silence at bay we made conversation about
things that neither of us was particularly interested in while
Mrs. Favor served us tea and cookies. Thornton Wilder had
been one of his French department colleagues for a while, he
said, and he told me how the great man would sit at his classroom table pounding it with his fist and shouting "Education
for sale!!"

I went to see him at the Exeter hospital after his final stroke,
but I don't think he knew I was there. He looked tiny and gray
in his crank bed with his teeth out, and I recited the Lord's
Prayer over him. When he died a day or so later, Mrs. Favor
asked me to conduct his service at a funeral home in
Portsmouth.

He had no friends in Exeter as far as I could tell nor did any
old ones show up from anywhere else, so there was no one present except for his cousin and me and a couple of undertakers.
And of course Boom Boom himself. I had never seen a dead
body at such close range before, and the sight unnerved me,
especially since the place where the undertakers told me to
stand was almost on top of him. There he lay in his box, all
brushed and combed and powdered, wearing a pair of check-
ered trousers bolder than anything I had ever seen him in
before and a rather loud tweed jacket and Brooks Brothers tie.
They had also put his glasses on—a pair of heavily horn-

rimmed spectacles that gave him an uncharacteristically stern and threatening look as if at any moment he might sit up and ask me to conjugate the present subjunctive of *avoir*. As I read the service, it was as hard for me to look at my old teacher lying there as it was to avoid looking at him.

His burial directly afterward took place at a cemetery on a bluff overlooking the sea with the same little group standing around with collars up and hands in pockets. There was a stiff breeze coming up off the water that would have blown his pearl-gray fedora into the next county and made his bright little paper-correcting eyes water behind those fierce glasses.

During that first homesick Lawrenceville year there had been a map of Europe on the wall of his classroom with something or other tacked to it so that the word *Spain* was reduced to *pain*, and he told us once with an embarrassed little titter that the verb *patiner*, to skate, was French slang for *to neck*, and I wondered if that was something he could ever conceivably have done himself. The closest he ever came to it may have been at a cocktail party we gave at Stone Cottage once when he got so carried away that he ended up with somebody's secretary sitting in his lap with too much lipstick on and her hair frizzed.

My prayer for him all these years later is that as he makes his way through the Elysian Fields he may somehow run into those handsome boys he had pictures of in his living room all those years ago, and that he may be able at last to embrace them without guilt or shame.

∽

Rod Emory, who taught history, came from East Paris, Maine, and like Boom Boom was a bachelor. He was a passionate lover of classical music with a large collection of records including some old 78s that broke if you so much as looked at them mixed in with a great number of the newly available 33s. He was a reserved, courteous, shy man but when something struck him funny, he would shake with uncontrollable laughter, and his face would go red as a boiled lobster.

Once at a dinner party we both attended he drank rather

more than he was used to and in the front hall where we were all making our polite farewells stumbled over a delicate little table that shattered into a thousand pieces as he fell on it. Several of us had to help him back to his dormitory and to bed, and for days afterward he was overwhelmed with horror at what he had done.

"The Fish" was what the boys called him, and when he asked a younger member of the history department one day *why* they called him the Fish, the answer he got was, "Because you look like a fish." And it was true—something about his wide mouth and the thrust of his jaw and the way his eyes seemed to be on different sides of his head.

A year or so later he was invited to another dinner, this time with just a colleague and his wife, who thought it would be entertaining to wear evening clothes for a change. When a full hour passed and Rod still hadn't shown up, the husband went to where he lived to see what had happened. He had apparently sat down in an armchair to put on his shoes, and then suffered a fatal heart attack. So there he was, all showered and shaved with his black tie tied and his thin hair brushed down sleek with his pink scalp showing through. His record player was running and the room was billowing with music.

ॐ

Tom Johnson, chairman of the English department, had the face of a Palmer Cox Brownie with pale, slightly protuberant eyes that every once in a while for no particular reason seemed to brim with tears and a cultivated voice so soft and hushed that it was as though he was speaking to you in the reading room of a library. When he was given the prestigious task of editing the great Harvard variorum edition of the poems of Emily Dickinson, he pinned up on the walls of his office a number of greatly magnified samples of her handwriting from various points in her life to help with dating poems that were undated. Since many of them were originally incorporated into letters to friends, he always dreamed that one day a new one might turn up between the pages of a book somewhere or tucked away at the back of a desk drawer.

At dinner once at his house I happened to mention that my Lawrenceville classmate Jimmy Merrill and I had been playing around with a Ouija board that summer, and Tom was immediately fascinated. Did I think it was conceivable that we could make contact with Emily? If we could get hold of a Ouija board somewhere, could he and I give it a try? I did better than that. In place of the commercial Parker Brothers kind, I made one then and there with a piece of brown wrapping paper marked with the twenty-six letters of the alphabet, the numbers 1 to 10, and the words Yes and No. For a planchette we used an upside-down teacup with the handle serving as pointer, and I sprinkled the paper with talcum powder to make it slide more easily.

We sat on opposite sides of the table each with the fingers of one hand resting lightly on the upside-down cup, and almost immediately it started swooping around with what seemed to be a will of its own. Who was there? we asked, and instantly it darted to the letters of her name. Tom was enraptured. Could Emily possibly tell us the whereabouts of any poems that hadn't been found yet? The answer was an immediate Yes. Could she go so far as to give us the names and addresses of the people who had them? Without hesitation the teacup again complied and spelled out some six or seven, all of them in New England and entirely believable. It zigzagged so rapidly that we barely had time to write each one down before it was on to the next. Then the single word GOODBYE.

Tom's problem was then how to explain himself without making the addressees take him for a screwball by explaining how he had found their names. What he finally did was write simply that he had reason to believe they might know the whereabouts of hitherto undiscovered Dickinson manuscripts and mailed his letters off the next day. Not only did he not receive a single answer, but one or two of them were returned stamped No such address, No such person, No such anything, and that was the end of that.

I can't remember the subject's ever coming up between the two of us again, but, if it did, I can imagine that vague, Brownie smile of his with the suggestion of tears in his pale eyes.

Hans Rastede taught German and was also in charge of one of the senior dorms. He had heavy-lidded cow eyes magnified by spectacles; a bony, sardonic face; and a habit of raising and lowering his eyebrows at unexpected moments as he talked, occasionally flashing a smile that seemed less a smile than a grimace of pain. He was convinced that someday he was going to have a major heart attack in the middle of the night and arranged with the boys whose rooms were on either side of his that if he rapped on the wall three times, they were to come running. He was always having elaborate physical examinations and after one of them told a group of us drinking coffee with him at the Jigger Shop that it had cost him a fortune and all he had found out was that he had an acid disposition. He always smoked with his coffee, holding his cigarette out at full arm's length in a lordly, expansive way and every now and then flicking the ash off onto the floor with a single tap of his forefinger. At the same time, with his other hand on the bridge of his nose between those great, half-closed eyes, he massaged his sinuses which he said were a constant source of torment to him. My friend Larry Hlavacek of the history department, who shared an apartment with me in Stone Cottage, did an imitation of him that was in great demand wherever he went.

I was taking Hans Rastede's dorm duty for him one evening, and when he returned to relieve me, he told me, raising and lowering his eyebrows, that he had just come from dinner with Albert Einstein and Thomas Mann. They were both in Princeton at the time, and he explained that he had been invited because they both liked having people around they could speak German to. It had been a lively and interesting evening, he said, and he was the one appointed to take them home when it was over. As they drove along through the night with himself at the wheel and the two immortals conversing in the back seat, he told me that it occurred to him that if they happened to have a smash-up, his name would appear with theirs in every paper in the country and for a few moments he would be as famous as they were.

His one other brush with fame, he said on some other occasion, occurred during his youth when a play he had written was produced on Broadway. All I can remember his saying about it was that the last scene took place outdoors on a summer night. There was a great tree of some kind at center stage with the moon shining down through the branches and fireflies flickering in the darkness. He said he had intended it to be very moving, and he himself had been very moved as he sat there watching it. But that was not the way it affected the audience, he said, gazing at me through the smoke of his cigarette. They thought it was funny and laughed, and the play closed after only that one performance.

The last time I saw him was after his retirement. A Lawrenceville classmate of mine and I were spending a few days in Bermuda when we got wind somehow that he was there too, staying at the St. George Hotel, a huge, cheerless place with an indoor pool that smelled of chlorine and a nine-hole golf course and not much to recommend it otherwise except for a sweeping view of St. George's harbor. Hans had a small, bare room toward the end of a long corridor on the ground floor, and his door was open to let in some air. He was sitting in his pajama pants bare from the waist up and glistening with sweat. He looked bony and putty-colored and was full of complaints. The food was inedible and the service a bad joke. The heat was terrible, and he couldn't get anybody to bring him an electric fan. And as usual his sinuses were giving him hell.

I couldn't tell whether he was glad we'd come or hoping we'd soon go. But he brightened visibly when we invited him to have dinner with us the next day at the Coral Beach club, and when the time came, he rose to the occasion. He looked better in a jacket and tie than he had in his pajama bottoms, and over a rum swizzle or two he told us a number of witty, vitriolic anecdotes about faculty members we had all known.

When it came time for him to go home, we got him a taxi. It was a convertible with the top down, and my last glimpse of

him was sitting in the back seat with his cigarette hand
extended regally at full length into the night. He said he had
enjoyed seeing us, and I was sure that it was true. The air was
soft and fragrant as he drove away, and there were fireflies twin-
kling like stars in the darkness around him.

The star of the show was of course Allan Vanderhoef Heely, the
headmaster, who was in his forties when I first met him. He
was the most articulate man I have ever known and in many
ways the most elegant. Whether he was delivering a baccalau-
reate address or making conversation at a dinner party or dis-
cussing life with a small boy at a baseball game, he always spoke
in sentences. He loved words, loved especially discovering new
ones—I remember to this day the pleasure it gave him to introduce me to "abdominous"—and used them with skill and verve
but always for the purpose of saying precisely what he meant
rather than just for effect. He had a husky, even-toned voice
and a rapid *rat-tat-tat* of a laugh except when something particularly delighted him in which case it became a single explosive
Hah! People said that he had a silver plate in his skull from
where his fontanelle had not closed over during infancy and
that he wore a flap of toupee to cover it, but if so you would
never have guessed it. Some people also said that his handsome,
patrician wife, Pattie, was a little dull-witted, but the truth of
the matter was that she was a woman of great charm and wit
whose vagueness and occasional non sequiturs had nothing to
do with dullness but were caused by deafness she was too proud
to do anything about or admit.

He was a very reserved man who did not let himself be
known easily, but somehow or other he managed to have all of
himself present in everything I ever heard him say or saw him
do. You always came upon him whole, and when he gave you
his attention, the gift was complete. Even at large school gath-
erings, besieged on all sides by alumni and faculty, students
and parents, he was never vague or desultory and never once
did I hear him be rude, although on occasion he could be

stunningly direct such as the time he was visiting us in Vermont when I asked him if he'd like to drive to the top of the hill to see the view, and his answer was, "I hate views. What I'd like is a very dry martini." Or his saying at a faculty meeting the day before school reopened one fall, "Gentlemen, never forget that when you enter your classrooms for the first time tomorrow you may very well find yourself in the presence of your intellectual superiors."

No matter how briefly you saw him, he left you with the feeling that you had genuinely met. He spoke with candor and listened with courtesy. He expected the best from you and thereby tended to evoke the best. You felt he was ready to forgive you for almost anything except being tasteless or dull, and he did not suffer fools gladly. He took special delight in two kinds of people—the very clever and the very natural—and also in the book of Job and *Alice in Wonderland*. He enjoyed playing the piano at Sunday coffee hours after morning chapel and relished good food and drink served with ceremony. Maybe what delighted him most was bright young seniors all brushed and combed and putting their best feet forward.

There was something of Caesar in his autumn-colored face—his profile blunt and imperious, his forehead high, his cleft chin firm and determined. When he walked around the campus in his English tweeds, he carried his head erect as a soldier's with his glance directed so straight and unwaveringly ahead of him that you felt if a circus elephant were suddenly to fall in step at his side, he wouldn't even notice.

More than anything else, it was from Allan Heely that generations of us learned for the first time in our lives what it was in the fullest sense of the word to be a *gentleman*.

∾

My father died only four years before I started out at Lawrenceville in the fall of 1940, but as far as I know I never thought about him or mourned him or was able even to remember what he looked like or the sound of his voice. Nor did I ever think either that there among the tall trees and brownstone buildings and green lawns the most precious treasure I was to find was the whole flawed and touching motley of fathers who in all likelihood themselves never thought for a moment that I would go on remembering them in richest detail and loving them for decades to come.

Bulletin Board

The one that hangs in my office is a hodgepodge. "Bulletin board" suggests something urgent and last minute whereas absolutely nothing I have on mine could conceivably be called either—quiescent and out of date would be more accurate. There are pictures mostly, added at different times and for different reasons over the years. Some of them are hiding or half hiding others beneath them. There is no rhyme or reason to them, no unifying theme. In some cases I can't remember why I chose them.

The one most likely to catch your eye first is a striking magazine photograph of the novelist and longtime literary editor of *The New Yorker*, William Maxwell. He is in his nineties with his crippled, arthritic hands side by side over the lower half of his face as though to stifle a cry. His eyes are narrowed, tragic, his brow creased, the background dark as night. Some people who knew him said he was a saint. They said if you told him your troubles, often tears would come to his eyes.

I never met him, but we exchanged a few letters toward the end of his life. In my first one I told him how enormously I admired *Time Will Darken It*, and he wrote back, "*Time Will*

Darken It is my cross-eyed child. When it first appeared I can't tell you how many dear friends wrote to say they disliked it intensely. . . . When I sat down to work, I would ask myself which of my characters had not been talking to each other and then put them in the same room. Fortunately, they were all talkative. . . . Your liking for the book has made me particularly happy."

Later I asked him about one of his most touching and unforgettable characters, Madame Straus-Muguet who appears in *The Chateau* as an old woman whom the narrator and his wife meet in France on their honeymoon. In one scene she comes to the Paris railway station to see them off, and "For reasons there was now no chance of their knowing," he writes, "she clung to them, hurrying along beside the slowly moving train, waving to them, calling goodbye. When she could no longer find them among the other heads and waving arms they could see her, still waving her crumpled handkerchief, old, forsaken, left in her own sad city, where the people she knew did not know her, and her stories were not believed even when they were true."

"Madame Straus-Muguet," he told me, "is based on a Frenchwoman we knew in the 1940s and '50s named Madame Schmidt-Mourguès. Not that that answers your question." Nor did it, of course, but as if by way of compensation he added, "To the best of my knowledge, I should say recollection, we haven't met face to face. But your letters have been so kind that they have left me with a feeling that we not only know each other but are friends."

It is a scandal that so few people even know his name let alone that he was one of the greatest, most human, wisest American writers of the twentieth century. Whenever I appear on some public platform or other I am invariably asked what writers I particularly admire, and when I ask how many in the audience of say two or three hundred have ever heard of him, usually no more than six or seven of them raise their hands.

His first novel, *Bright Center of Heaven*, written in 1934 when he was twenty-six, is derivative and unconvincing, but in

They Came Like Swallows, based on memories of his mother's
death from Spanish influenza during the epidemic of 1918
when he was ten, he is clearly and powerfully speaking in his
own true voice out of the deepest truth of his own life as he
continued to do from that time forward. When I asked him if
he could account for such a major change in such a brief time,
he referred me to his introduction to the Modern Library edition of *They Came Like Swallows*, which as far as I can see
doesn't answer the question at all.

The greatest bond between us didn't emerge until his letter
thanking me for a copy I'd sent him of a short novel of mine
called *The Wizard's Tide* in which I tried to tell the story of my
father's suicide from the point of view of the ten-year-old I was
when it happened. "I was struck with how original the
approach is," he wrote, "and also by the clear correspondence
with certain details of my life that I have never written about.
It brought back vividly the dreadful morning when my grandmother gathered me into her lap and my aunt told my brother
and me that our mother had died."

In the case of my brother and me, we didn't have to be told
because from the window of our second-floor bedroom we
could look down at the driveway and see what had happened
for ourselves.

❧

With a corner of it hidden by a mostly illegible postcard from
our then nine-year-old grandson Dylan, there is another postcard of the great African American soprano, Jessye Norman.
She is holding her hands palm to palm, fingers splayed, at her
throat. She is wearing a dark cloak pulled up in folds around
her chin. Her mouth is open wide. Her eyes are closed. Her
great mane of hair flies out behind her like one of the Furies.
Her expression is ecstatic. I can all but hear her singing the final
words of Richard Strauss's heartbreaking "September"—
"*Langsam tut er die müdgewordenen Augen zu*" (slowly he closes
his wearying eyes) with the five syllables of *müdgewordenen*
zigzagging softly through the air like autumn leaves. One

spring afternoon we sat next to each other at an endless Yale commencement where we were both to receive honorary doctorates, and when we stood to sing a hymn, sharing the hymnal between us, I wondered if she would take the top of my head off with that extraordinary voice. She sang it, instead, as quietly as a child.

A few years ago my friend and former Exeter student John Irving sent me a photograph of himself receiving an Oscar for the screenplay he wrote of *Cider House Rules*. He is wearing a black suit and black shirt and stands against a black background holding his Oscar at hip level. Lit from below, his face is a mask of astonishment and horror, the frown lines deep between his eyes and the corners of his mouth drawn downward. He could be Jack the Ripper caught red-handed. On a slow afternoon he sells as many copies of a single book as I have sold of all the books I have ever written, but I have found it in my heart to forgive him, and we remain good friends even so. In one of his novels the character of a minister based loosely on me turns out to be the narrator's father, and during the question-and-answer session following some lecture of mine, I was asked if John Irving was really my son. I like to believe that my answer was yes.

From the cover of *The Princeton Alumni Weekly*, my old creative writing teacher, Richard P. Blackmur, looks out quizzically and with faint amusement through his dark-rimmed glasses. Once at an alcoholic New Year's Eve party during my undergraduate years he trapped me against a wall with one hand propped against the wall on either side of my head and after telling me I had "a way with words," went on to say, referring to another of his students, "I would invest in Berlind, but I would bet on Buechner." He also said that I would always "float to the top." Just how he intended me to take these ambiguous utterances I remain uncertain to this day. But when it came to his parting words, there seemed to be only one way. I would die of prostate cancer at the age of fifty-six, he told me, and until that fatal date came and went, I watched for it uneasily out of the corner of one eye.

And then a miscellany:

The Queen Mum on her one hundredth birthday. She is wearing a triple strand of pearls, an off-the-face white-brimmed hat with a little half veil. In one hand she is holding a big inflated plastic heart and in the other a single flower that a small child seems to have just presented her. She looks her age but is smiling graciously, the only member of that dismal family I could ever muster any affection for.

Frank Tracy Griswold, presiding bishop of the Episcopal Church, is smiling benignly in his dog collar and steel-rimmed glasses, that strikingly intelligent, articulate, sweet-tempered man. He told me that once when he was taking a shower, he distinctly heard a voice from somewhere saying, "Why do you take your sins so much more seriously than I do?" His first reaction, he said, was to burst into laughter. His second was to burst into tears.

Presidents Clinton, G. H. W. Bush, Reagan, Carter, and Ford are sitting with their wives at the funeral of Richard Nixon looking genuinely moved and touchingly unpresidential.

My cousin and almost exact contemporary, Tom Buechner, chose to wear a dinner jacket for his self-portrait which he sent me a postcard of. He looks quite forbidding with his full white beard and somber frown. His father was my father's youngest brother, and like him, eight years later, committed suicide. We have seen each other only sporadically since the golden days of our boyhood, but bonds were forged between us then that haunt us still, and though we are on the verge of turning eighty, we remain the keepers of secrets known only to each other. He once said to me years ago, "I wish someday we could meet as strangers," and I knew exactly what he meant.

Another Episcopal priest glances sideways in more or less the direction of a stunning black-and-white photograph of

Princess Diana in a low-cut, long-sleeved white blouse and dark slacks. Bob Clayton was his name, and for some nine years he let me use a Sunday school room in the parish house of his church for writing my books, *Godric* and most of the Bebb tetralogy among them. You never knew what state you would find him in—full of nervous energy and ebullience and chatter one day and on other days lost in some deep, dark place within himself. I suppose the reason he found it so nearly impossible to talk about anything other than the most superficial matters was that he was terrified of what he might find deeper down.

When I discovered that every day at eight he celebrated morning prayers all by himself, I started joining him at them—one week he would be the minister and I the congregation and the next week the other way around—until in time I realized that it had become the most important part of my day and also, as it turned out, of his. One afternoon, apropos of nothing we had been talking about, he told me that my being there with him all those nine years had saved his life, and I realized with a little jolt that he was speaking literally. If so, it was the last thing I had ever in any sense thought of myself as doing. I don't even know how to save my own life but it had happened and it was a gift of sheer grace to both of us.

Henry James and his brother William look grim and uncomfortable in each other's presence, Henry in an oddly flamboyant bow tie and William positively sacerdotal in his high starched collar. I met an acquaintance of Henry's once who told me that he had the unnerving habit of taking hold of you by the lapels while he talked and of drawing you closer and closer as he worked through one of his labyrinthine sentences until by the time he finally came to the end, your noses were all but touching.

Below the James brothers, Laurel and Hardy are side by side in their derby hats, each with a cautionary finger to his lips. It was Dick Van Dyke who wrote that the secret of their enduring popularity is that through all of Hardy's browbeating and all of Laurel's falsetto, hair-twirling tears, you knew that they loved each other.

The only worldly possessions that Mahatma Gandhi owned at the time of his death are laid out on three stairs, including his spectacles; a pair of sandals; the kind of little see-no-evil, hear-no-evil, speak-no-evil monkeys you could buy at a dime store; and an empty bowl.

There is also the typed copy of an epitaph our friends Cot and Anne Campbell came across one day in some cemetery:

Damien Ryan Parlor

Child of Light
Bridge in the Universe
So Dearly Loved
Danced in Sunlight
Floated on Moonbeams
Dreamed on Clouds
Laughed Soaring Hawk Songs
Cried Brilliant Rainbows
Reached for the Stars

August 1974–September 1984

A Boy who could pet bees
I love you Damie

The Laughter Barrel

My first meeting with Maya Angelou took place at the Trinity Institute in New York City where we had both been invited to come and in effect tell our stories before a large audience of Episcopal clergy who were there more or less to have their batteries recharged. I no longer remember how it was I went about it—I think I may have read from one of my books—but one way or another I described something of my background and told how despite having grown up in a family without any interest in religion in general or church in particular I found myself little by little so drawn to the Christian faith I knew almost nothing about that in my middle twenties I enrolled at Union Theological Seminary in its heyday and was eventually, to nobody's surprise more than my own, ordained as a Presbyterian minister.

After I finished, the same man who had introduced me proceeded to introduce Maya Angelou. They would now hear from her, he said, a very different story from the one they had just heard from me, and he had every reason to believe such would be the case. She was a woman, and I was a man. She was black, and I was white. Though my family was often hard pressed for money those Depression years, in comparison with her I had grown up in the lap of luxury, always living in pleasant places and going to good schools whereas she had been brought up by her grandmother in the rear of the black people's store she ran in Stamps, Arkansas, during the worst days of redneck racism. But even as Fred Burnham was saying how different our two stories had been, I could see her shaking her head from side to side, and when she took her place at the lectern the first thing she did was say that he was wrong.

"No," she said, "Frederick Buechner and I have exactly the same story."

She was right, of course. At the deepest level the story of any one of us is the story of all of us. We all have the same dreams, the same doubts, the same fears in the night. Her words brought sudden tears to my eyes.

And then she went on with her talk whose title if I remember rightly was "The Accessibility of God," and I remember the way she drew the word "accessibility" out to its full length so that each of its six syllables got its full due.

She was an extraordinary woman to behold, larger than life, with a smile that lit up the room and the dignity of a queen. Elegantly dressed with strings of beads around her neck and on her head a turban of brightly dyed African cloth, she made it clear right away that she was going to go wherever her heart took her. If it seemed the right thing to do, she would suddenly break into a scrap of song or spiritual in a voice that welled up out of the deepest truth of who she was. Sometimes, if she thought it fitted in, she would tell a story or recite a poem. At one point she told us something about slavery days that I had never come across before.

On certain plantations, she said, it was forbidden for slaves to laugh as they worked, presumably because the masters were afraid that if it ever turned into laughter at *them*, the whole system might start to crumble. But if they couldn't contain themselves, she said, what they would do was go over to some barrel that was standing around and under the pretext of looking for something reach down into it as far as they could and let great peals ring out where nobody could hear them.

At the opening worship service earlier in the day there had been a procession of church dignitaries, and she continued by saying that as they had come parading down the aisle rigged out in their most elaborate ecclesiastical vestments and regalia, she had had an almost irresistible urge to duck off into some out-of-the-way corner somewhere—and at that point she interrupted herself by bending over double and letting fly with a cascade of laughter that no one who heard her is ever likely to forget.

Years later I stayed with her for a few days in Winston-Salem, North Carolina, where she had a many-roomed house filled with art she had collected or been given over the years together with photographs of friends like Nelson Mandela and James Baldwin and Oprah Winfrey, and shelf after shelf of books. She also had a number of other African Americans helping run things for her there, but never for an instant did she treat them like servants, addressing them always as Mrs. Thomas, Miss Stuckey, Mr. Miles, just as they always addressed her as Dr. Angelou. It was as if they were all of them trying to make it up to each other for all the years they had been treated like dirt.

Toward the end of the day I was thinking of going to my room for a nap before dinner but somehow or other found myself instead sitting with her in a little gazebo overlooking her garden, and with the spring afternoon soft and fragrant about us, I listened to her talk as randomly and easily as she had at the Trinity Institute while we sipped the scotch that Mrs. Thomas kept us supplied with. She is as good a listener as she is a talker, but I kept mostly silent so as not to interrupt her wonderful, lazy progress from one thing to another.

She seems able to quote by memory from virtually everything she has ever read, and somewhere along the way, apropos of I've no idea what, she recited a poem by Edna St. Vincent Millay, titled "Conscientious Objector," which moved me deeply.

And then, "I believe I'll have just one more, Mrs. Thomas," she said, "only this time don't bother with the ice and water, dear," and heaven only knows what she turned to next, or what I did, though I do remember that at some point she said in a slow, pensive way as if it was only then occurring to her that she believed that, given the chance, we could be real friends. I replied that I thought we were that already, but she said, "No, I mean *real* friends," and if we didn't live so many miles apart, and if she wasn't so busy being a celebrity and I being whatever I am, I think she may have been right.

In any case as we sat there I had the feeling that even if we never set eyes on each other again, in some soft, shadowy way we had left a lasting mark on each other. For a few moments, with the dusk beginning to gather, our two stories merged like raindrops on a window pane.

The Five Sisters

The first place I can remember more than just glimpses of was the New York apartment of my Buechner grandparents at 940 Park Avenue on the corner of Park and East Eighty-first Street. I remember that it looked different to me from all the other apartment buildings—the stone squares it was faced with larger and smoother and tanner. I remember the doorman uniformed like a field marshal who helped tuck the fur-lined car robe about my grandmother's knees on winter days when the chauffeur came to take her somewhere. I remember the chauffeur—a German named Werner who my grandmother said was fresh as paint and who spent a great deal of his time smoking cigarettes in the kitchen while he waited to be summoned. He had a son about my age named Hans, and I remember how for some forgotten reason he and my younger brother Jamie and I were all picking blackberries out in the country somewhere when Werner called out, "Reach for the big ones, Hans!" which remained a family byword for years afterward.

There was an abandoned Catholic convent a few blocks north on Madison Avenue if I remember rightly. It was a gloomy-looking place built of dark red brick with broken panes here and there where the windows hadn't been boarded over and a scruffy yard littered with Dixie cup lids and gum wrappers and empty cigarette packs tossed over the spear-shaped palings of the high fence that surrounded it. A few blocks farther north still, on Fifth Avenue with its back to the park, was the Metropolitan Museum of Art which from the age of ten or so on my cousin Tommy and I used to spend hours in—the high-ceilinged room hung with banners where the knights in armor were, the Pompeian garden with beautiful young men and women of polished marble standing naked around a shallow pool beneath a glass ceiling that let the silvery daylight in, and a reconstructed Egyptian tomb just big enough for two or three people to squeeze into at the same time. It had a kind of dimly sour smell to it that I can still conjure up and assumed was the smell of antiquity.

It was on the second floor where the paintings were, however, that we spent most of our time, eventually bringing sketch pads and soft black pencils with us which we had to get official permission to use for making copies of pictures that appealed to us—I remember especially one of Rembrandt's marvelous old women with a waxy, wrinkled face surrounded by an enormous ruff, and some early-nineteenth-century New York patrician in brass buttons and a high white stock with a face that reminded me of Edna May Oliver. We lost all track of time as we worked, and our copies were good enough so that sometimes people would pause to watch over our shoulders, giving me my first taste of an audience not just of admiring relatives but of strangers who were simply interested in what I was doing for its own sake.

Those museum expeditions of Tommy's and mine were also the first experience either of us had had until then of being off on our own with nobody to know what we were up to so that there was a clandestine air about it almost, an unspoken sense of excitement at the thought of what we might take it into our heads to do together next. It was alone in each other's presence that we got our first glimpse of how we were different from the way our fathers had been at our age—not going out into the park to kick a ball around or roller-skate on the twisting asphalt paths or row on the lake but discovering a rich and private world of our own where a bond was established between us that was to become increasingly complex as the years went by, even though our lives took us in different directions and our meetings became fewer and further between. "Island encounters" is what Tommy called them.

The other world we shared, of course, was the apartment at 940 Park. The living room was the heart of it—the *Herrenstube*, as it was called by Rosa, who wouldn't have dreamed of sitting down in it when she was summoned to discuss some household matter. There was a Steinway grand in it, a gift to my grandmother from her father, old Herman Balthazar Scharmann, who had given one like it to each of his five daughters when they were married, and a circular mahogany center table on which stood a white alabaster filigree model of the Taj Mahal under a glass dome, another gift from her father who had brought it back from a world tour he made after his wife's death. My grandmother's chair was in a corner by the window looking out on Eighty-first Street and next to it her sewing stand with hinged lids on either side that opened up on little sliding shelves of silk thread of every conceivable color, spools of cotton, crochet hooks, packets of needles, thimbles, a pair of gilt sewing scissors made like a bird with a long sharp beak. A Tiffany standing lamp with a fringed shade of green silk gave light over her shoulder, and nearby, on a tall fluted pedestal, there was a marble bust of the goddess Aphrodite whose bare breasts I remember once reaching up to touch because with my grandfather's eye upon me from the other side of the room I couldn't think of anything else to do.

My grandmother virtually lived in that chair by the window, and on Saturday afternoons would listen to the opera from it on her tinny little radio that she kept on the windowsill at her elbow. Wagner was her favorite, and she knew the score so well that from time to time she would sing along for a little in a delicate, high-pitched voice that seemed incongruous from someone as large as she eventually became. It

reached the point where she didn't so much sit in her chair—
unable to bend at the waist because she virtually no longer had
a waist to bend at—as more or less lie in it with her legs
stretched straight out on a needlepoint footstool and her
sewing things resting on the broad shelf of her bosom. I picture her there particularly on winter afternoons at dusk with
the sad, soft honking of the rush hour traffic heading home up
Park Avenue eight stories below.

My grandfather's chair was in the opposite corner with a
wrought-iron smoker's stand beside it and his pipe rack within
reach, but even when he was sitting there, the heart and com-
mand center of the room remained my grandmother even
when she happened to be somewhere else. Once his silk
importing business went under in '29, she was the one who
with a generous legacy from her father held the purse strings
and called the shots. It was her birthday that we forgot at our
peril. It was she whom her three sons phoned virtually every
day of their lives and whose hard-drinking, heavy-smoking,
mannish daughter married a gentle, effeminate young man
solely for the purpose of getting out from under her thumb. It
was she who rode herd on Rosa and Anna Pelkoffer, the German sisters who had worked for my grandmother since my
father's childhood, and she who excoriated Werner from the
back seat of her limousine if for one reason or another his driving didn't please her. When she herself was at the wheel, if the
car in front of her was not going fast enough to suit her, she
would come up from behind and bump it a few times.

My grandmother was the one who kept track of all our com-
ings and goings and was sure something unspeakable had happened every time one of us came home late or failed to show up
just when and where she expected us. When the unspeakable
things finally did happen—my father's suicide in 1936 followed by my grandfather's death five days later and the suicide
of Uncle Tom (Tommy's father) a few years afterward—she was
the one hit hardest and yet, maybe because of those long years
of preparation, instead of being destroyed or embittered she
emerged somehow softened, muted, like the horns on Park

Avenue so that in her last years it was less the Valkyries' fierce war cries that make me think of her than Wotan's farewell or the Liebestod.

But after the unspeakable things no less than before them, she continued to hold sway at 940 Park like Queen Victoria, whom she slightly resembled, at Windsor Castle, and never more resplendently than at the great kaffeeklatsches that she held for her four sisters and such of their progeny and hers as felt up to attending. Rosa, her usual workaday uniform replaced by a magnificent wine-colored one with white collar and cuffs and a lacy, starched apron, received them as they arrived a few at a time in the hall where the grandfather's clock stood with its narrow, arched door of beveled glass and not only ponderously rang the hour in a resounding, subterranean bass like Mozart's Commendatore but also showed the phases of the moon moving slowly across its face.

There was a large gilt mirror for the ladies to arrange their hair in, a tapering, square umbrella stand full of my grandfather's walking sticks, and a narrow wood bench with arabesques and heraldic emblems burned into it by whichever one of the sisters had learned how. Rosa helped them off with their furs and coats and when the hall closet was full laid them out carefully in the guest room on the enormous, creaky bed with an unyielding hair mattress that Tommy and I sometimes shared as, later in our adolescence, we shared the twin beds in Aunt Betty's unoccupied room that were pushed so tightly together that we had neither the independence of a single nor the adventure and warmth of a double.

On kaffeeklatsch days Mrs. Wilms, the laundress, was called on to help Anna in the kitchen with the endless trays of little triangular sandwiches, pastries, whipped cream and strawberries, and God knows what-all else that Rosa and some other maid taken on especially for the purpose edged their way through the overstuffed ladies to serve. I remember the rich, bitter smell of the coffee, the tinkling of silver against porcelain, the radiance of all those silk-shaded lamps lit at once, and, most of all, the voices speaking now in English and now in

German, the rise and the fall of them, the squeals of laughter, the little explosions of surprise or indignation as they brought each other up to date, asked about each other's families, shared ancient jokes and memories, and above all else argued with each other so noisily that according to legend some stranger attending for the first time asked what on earth they were fighting about only to be told that when the Scharmann sisters got together it was always like that. They weren't fighting. They were klatsching. Like the big-busted divas in Wagner, they were merely raising their voices in fierce and passionate song.

It is Tante Annie who comes to mind first for some reason, not a Scharmann by birth but the wife of my grandmother's brother Herman—a short, plump, rosy-cheeked woman with snowy hair piled high like whipped cream, a string or two of pearls around her neck, and her small feet in patent leather pumps. Like most of the others she does not leave her hat with Rosa upon arriving but continues to wear it throughout. There is something about her that conjures up Schraffts, that fancy string of ice cream shop restaurants where ladies could have lunch or tea served by waitresses uniformed like their maids at home or sit on high stools at the marble-topped counter hoping nobody they knew would notice and avoiding their reflection in the long mirror as they bent over hot fudge sundaes or brownies à la mode. Like a box of expensive chocolates, she is done up elegantly with a sheen of broad satin ribbon here, a glint of gold or silver there, the sense of something rich and irresistible inside. It was she and her husband who fell heir to the portraits of the senior Scharmanns.

My great-grandfather, in his, looks splenetic and massive with his grizzled Buffalo Bill moustache and goatee and his pince-nez aglitter. He is holding his long-ashed, smoking cigar in his left hand with the right one resting on his paunch where his watch chain glimmers in the shadows. Frieda, his long-suffering wife, is all in black with a circular pearl brooch at her throat and her shirtfront a cascade of ruffles and jet beading. She was painted posthumously at her husband's behest, and the trace of sadness and apprehension in her faint smile suggests that if it weren't for the honor of the thing she would as soon have been allowed to rest in peace.

Aunt Frida, the oldest of their five daughters, was born before her father's brewery had made him the rich man he eventually became so that she did not receive the expensive education enjoyed by her sisters and spent the rest of her life resenting what she had missed and trying to compensate for it by studying such things as the Italian language and the piano which she continued to practice on daily in her lonely apartment at the Hotel Pierre until her fingers became so crippled with arthritis that she could no longer manage it. She was only twenty-seven when her husband abandoned her and their two sons, and after a ten-year attempt at reconciliation, during which she apparently did all she could to humiliate him for how he had humiliated her, they were finally divorced at a time when such a thing was almost unheard of.

I remember her as a wiry, grim little woman who, fixing you with a gimlet stare, would speak her mind with terrifying frankness, and always referred to me as "The Poet" with a mixture of irony and grudging admiration. It is hard to picture her feasting on Zimmtsterne, Anisplätzschen, Käsekuchen, cucumber sandwiches and gossiping with the rest of them, but year after year she came even so and for all I know got some kind of grim pleasure out of being the one intellectual among them.

The next in line was Aunt Emma Zinsser with her bright little eyes, roses in her cheeks, and a patrician accent that was unlike that of any of her sisters. She married well and lived at Hastings on the Hudson in a large white house with a drawing room that looked down over a lovely stretch of the river and a children's playhouse modeled on the big one. Despite falling down the elevator shaft when she stepped into it with an armful of dry-cleaning to take down to the kitchen without seeing that the car was not there, she survived well into her eighties by keeping in trim with yoga exercises that included standing on her head for an extended period every day.

Toward the end of her life she started telling hair-raising tales of her father's despotism such as how once at dinner when a son-in-law didn't leap up instantly to fetch whatever it was he had asked for, he brought his fist down on the table with such violence that cups rattled in their saucers and everybody sat there in stunned silence. Yet all of his daughters had so revered and loved him that even years after his death their eyes would fill with tears at the mere mention of his name.

Aunt Emma herself had two daughters, one of whom married Lewis Douglas, the American ambassador to England under Truman as well as Franklin Roosevelt's first budget director, and the other John McCloy, who was the high commissioner of Germany after the Second World War and later a member of the Warren Commission to investigate the assassination of John F. Kennedy.

There is a picture of all five of the sisters taken outdoors at a family wedding in 1940 when their ages ranged from fifty-two (Marie) to seventy-three (Frida), and Aunt Emma is seated in the middle in the one comfortable chair. The others are in dark dresses wearing hats, but Aunt Emma, hatless, has on a full-length white gown with a long-fringed white shawl draped over her shoulders. Her hair also is white, her faint smile is gracious, and she seems to be unquestionably the queen among them.

The next in line was Aunt Tony, who married a Jewish friend of the family at a time when it was considered simply the marriage of one German American to another. Uncle Julius Liebman became head of the Rhinegold brewery, and they lived in a spacious Fifth Avenue apartment overlooking Central Park and spent summers in a rambling white house on the sound in Bayport, Long Island. In addition to tennis, they also had a clipped green croquet court, and when Aunt Tony and my grandmother played on it, they did not hold the mallet in both hands, striking the ball directly in front of them, but in the right hand only, striking the ball from the side because that was the way they had done it in the days when they had needed the left hand to keep their long skirts from getting in the way.

Uncle Julius was an elegant old gentleman with a silvery goatee, a sandpapery voice, and blue eyes, and Aunt Tony wore steel-rimmed glasses and was very earnest about almost everything. I remember her once giving my brother Jamie and me some little china animal that couldn't have cost more than ten cents at Woolworth's and spending at least twenty minutes showing us in exhaustive detail how skillfully and painstakingly it had been made so that we would be sure to take good care of it. When her only grandchild was born, she encouraged her son to change his name to Leland so that the little girl would not be discriminated against in a world that had become increasingly anti-Semitic since her grandparents' day.

Of their own four children, one son and one daughter grew up to be successful doctors, but two other sons were handicapped, one of them so seriously that he had to be institutionalized from early childhood. The other, though sharp as a fox, had such psychological problems that his parents took him to Vienna to be psychoanalyzed by the great Dr. Freud himself. When this failed to cure him, he was committed to McLean's Hospital outside of Boston, where once a year for the rest of his life he contrived to escape for just long enough to demonstrate to the world that he remained there not because he was forced to but by his own free choice.

The youngest of the five Scharmann sisters was Marie, with the accent on the first syllable in the German fashion, who came to be known as Aunt Budlein. She had heavy-lidded eyes, a belly laugh deep as a man's, and though as a girl she was admired for her hourglass figure, she grew to be even fatter than my grandmother. She married a man named Carl Zellner—son of a well-known Brooklyn cameo-cutter—who was short and bald and limped badly because of a shriveled leg. When he and Aunt Marie got going at each other, they made a great comic team, and I remember her telling him one day as they were getting ready to leave my grandmother's apartment after a visit that she wished he wouldn't wear his best overcoat so often because she was planning to have him buried in it, and though I don't remember his rejoinder, I can still hear the cackle of his laugh blending with the bass drum of hers. As far as I know, he never had to work for a living— old Herman Balhasar Scharmann, my great-grandfather, left all his children enough in the way of money and Brooklyn real estate to make that unnecessary—but his life was memorable for two major achievements.

One of them was the scale model of a coach he had made, which every time we went to see them was trotted out for our delectation. The tiny brass door handles, the fringed window shades, the decorated spokes of the wheels, the upholstered seats inside, the little steps that could be lowered and raised, the shafts for the horses, the hinges of the doors—not only had he made every bit and piece of it by hand but he had made most of the tools needed for its construction as well. No matter how often he had shown it to us before, it was unveiled with such ceremony each time that we never failed to be awed.

His other major achievement was his famous old-fashioneds which he assembled with no less care than the immortal coach—the lump of sugar crushed at the bottom of the glass with a pestle, just the proper size dash of angostura bitters, the twelve-year-old bourbon, the cracked ice, and—his own special touch—some kind of candied orange slices that came in a jar packed with sweet syrup that had to be carefully drained off when you removed them. And of course the single glistening maraschino cherry added last of all for panache.

One of his comparatively minor achievements worth mentioning was a brass cigarette box he gave us for a wedding present with my wife's monogram in raised copper letters on the lid. At some later date when my wife asked what kind of polish he would recommend for brightening it up a little, he was horrified. He said he had buried it for six months in the wet sand of the Long Island Sound at Sachem's Head so that the salt water would give it just the right patina, and it would be a tragedy to think of using any kind of polish whatever.

When my grandmother died in 1958 in her eighties, Aunt Marie was the only sister left to attend the burial of her ashes in the family plot in Greenwood Cemetery. It was the first such service I had ever conducted, having not even been ordained yet by then, and there were only a few of us present.

When it was over and we were getting ready to leave, she

hobbled up to me and spoke in a voice I can still hear. It was the voice of grim resignation and deep-drawn grief and also a kind of sardonic jab at God, whom none of the Scharmanns had much time for, for having blown it again.

"Well," she said, her great face wet with tears, "so that is that," and then went listing off on her cane through the weathered graves.

Gertrude Conover Remembers

"People talk about fallen-away Catholics," Gertrude Conover said, "and it has always struck me as an unfortunate turn of phrase. It makes them sound like autumn leaves blowing about helter skelter till somebody comes along and makes a bonfire out of them. I do not think of myself as a fallen-away theosophist but just as a theosophist who hasn't kept au courant with things the way I once did: a *lazy* theosophist. In my younger days I read a good deal of Madame Blavatsky and with her help made some quite significant little strides toward cosmic consciousness, but then early in my marriage to Harold Conover I hired a Swedish cook who looked much like her—dumpy and brooding and unwashed—and who turned out to be such a disaster that I transferred my negative feelings about her to poor Madame Blavatsky herself and more or less gave up reading her for good. The cook's name was Greta, and we kept finding her long dark hairs in the food.

"Well," she went on, "theosophists believe in reincarnation of course, and as far as I am concerned, they have hit the nail on the head. Life after life after life we keep coming back into the world, and each time we do, the kind of life we are born into is the result of the life we led before. That doesn't mean we are punished for being bad and rewarded for being good by some sort of cosmic policeman. It means simply that if we are cruel and hateful one time round, then the next time round the only kind of life we will be able to squeeze into—that we'll even be *interested* in squeezing into—will be the life of a sabre-toothed tiger, say, or a serial killer. Sow a thought and reap an action, they say. Sow an action and reap a habit. Sow a habit and reap a destiny. In other words, we have only ourselves to blame or thank for what becomes of us. It is like one of those boxes you give small children to play with that have differently shaped holes in the lid. If you've made yourself into a triangular shape, then of course the only hole you'll fit into is a triangular hole. My dear, that is the law of karma in a nutshell.

"Around and around you go on the wheel of life like riding a Ferris wheel at a county fair until finally you realize that the you that keeps on being born and dying over and over again doesn't really exist at all. It is like an ocean wave that thinks it is separate and distinct from the ocean. As soon as it sees the error of its ways, it sinks blissfully back into the great blue depths of nirvana which of course is just where it has been all along without realizing it."

At about this point Calloway came out through the French windows wearing the starched white jacket that made him look so black that like the Invisible Man there seemed to be nobody wearing it at all. He was carrying a silver tray with a plate of graham crackers on it which he passed to Bebb and Gertrude Conover and me to go with our iced tea. It was Gertrude Conover's belief that he had been a pharaoh in some earlier existence—"He had only to snap his fingers," I remember her saying once, "and both the Lower and Upper Kingdoms would snap to attention"—and although as far as I know, Calloway himself was unaware of his former glory, there was an undeniable kingliness about him as he passed among us like a shadow.

"Don't think it hasn't crossed my mind that I am just a dotty old woman, but I believe in past lives not merely because Madame Blavatsky did, not to mention any number of overweight swamis who look as if they have B.O. but because I remember a great many of my own past lives quite vividly. People ask me sometimes if it doesn't make me dizzy to carry so many of them around with me all the time, and of course the answer is that I don't. I don't even remember all the lives I've lived just as Gertrude Conover unless something happens to remind me. I go about my business like anybody else—whatever it is I spend my days doing. The telephone. Getting things *fixed*. Looking for my damned glasses. Until something stops me in my tracks like Proust with his tea cake or whatever it was, and all of a sudden I am a little bit of a thing again playing with my favorite doll. His name was Frank, and he had only one eye.

"Harold Conover played football at Princeton. It was the high point of his life, I think, and that is why like so many of those old grads he came back to live here as soon as he could. Once in a while I went to a game with him though I never understood what on earth was going on and invariably kept my eye on the one who was pretending to carry the ball instead of the one who was actually carrying it. The only part I really enjoyed was watching the crowd. Harold always brought a motoring robe with us that had belonged to his mother in the days when the chauffeur was separated from you by a pane of glass so you had to speak to him through a tube. It had her monogram on one side with a silky gray fur on the other, and we would sit with it over our knees on a crisp autumn afternoon. During the half a perfectly enormous man would walk out onto the field and lead the whole stadium in the Princeton song. The last part of it went 'For they shall give—while they shall live—three cheers—for old Nassau'—how could I ever forget it?—and all the old Princetonians and the young ones too would rise to their feet and slowly wave their hats back and forth across their chests to the solemn beat of it. My dear, the face of Harold Conover would be positively awash with tears.

"In any case, it was at one of those games that I noticed a girl sitting only a few seats away from us with her beau. He was a very good-looking boy with dark, straight eyebrows and teeth that 'seemed for laughing round an apple' like the soldier in Wilfred Owen's poem, and the girl was so lovely she quite took my breath away. I will not try to describe her, but as her beau bent down to light a cigarette out of the breeze—in those days absolutely everybody smoked because no one thought there was the least bit of harm in it—she leaned over and kissed him on the back of his neck. Suddenly at that very moment there came welling up in me an entire life I had lived in Elizabethan England.

"Well, there wasn't a single detail of it that didn't come welling up, even the name of the village where we lived—It was Shottery—and the smell of thatched roofs after a rain, and the clang of the church bells, and the careworn face of my mother. Someday perhaps I will tell you more about it, but what made me positively tremble as I sat there on that hard pink granite was the memory of a boy I had known when I was as young and lovely as that girl sitting there with a yellow chrysanthemum pinned to her coat. His name was Colin—he was some sort of cousin to the woman William Shakespeare got in a family way—and though we never married, we were lovers. He had pointy ears like a fawn and a limp from where a hay wain had once tipped over on him, but he was strong and fleet as a young hart—you see even now the old-fashioned words come back to me like hart and wain, like fleet—and we had to see each other secretly because my father was too poor to be able to give me a dowry and his family didn't want him to get mixed up with me.

"There was a tumbledown hut in the woods between our farms that nobody ever went near because a witch had lived in it once, and that is where we would meet. There were spiders and daddy longlegs and field mice coming in to build nests in the straw at the first sign of frost. Sometimes at dusk a nightingale would sing for us, and in springtime the whole floor of the woods was covered with bluebells and campion, and when we lay there in each other's arms, I think even the heart of the witch would have melted to see how much we loved each other and how innocent we were although if they had ever found us we would have been hauled into court because that was what they did in those days, and there would have been a perfectly dreadful row.

"Well, I won't tell you any more about Colin now because it is all water over the dam and what is the point, but I will say this. When I saw the girl with the chrysanthemum, I was all at once swept back into being the girl I had been all those lives ago—my name was Lettice, not with a *u* like the vegetable but with an *i*—and right there with everyone around me waving orange and black pennants I found myself sobbing like a child. It brings tears to my eyes even now.

"Harold Conover was an old bachelor in his seventies when I married him, and I was in my early fifties. It was more of a beautiful friendship than a romance, I suppose you might say, and we had almost twenty years together. A lot of it we spent traveling one place or another—I don't believe there was a world capital we didn't visit or a single famous museum. But we spent a lot of time right here at Revonoc too and every year threw a huge cocktail party at reunion time when the magnolias were out. We always had a tent put up in case it rained although as far as I can remember it never did.

"When nobody was around, we called each other Baby, and after he had his stroke I took care of him like a baby, he was so helpless, poor dear. He couldn't speak, but I could see in his eyes that he was thanking me every time I came into the room and trying to reach out his hand to me although it was all he could do just to raise it off the covers. All the nurses could see what was in his eyes too and commented on it. I still get Christmas cards from one or two of them.

"Now I will tell you something I have never told a living soul before because I feel we have known each other forever, and in your case, Leo, that is not far from the truth. There isn't a life I can remember that you didn't show up in somewhere along the line—all those lives stretching on and on like one of those fitting-room mirrors where you see yourself reflected again and again down an endless corridor.

"What I want to tell you is this. Here at Revonoc Harold Conover and I had separate bedrooms, and when it came time to retire, one of us would always come in to kiss the other good night, and then we would go our separate ways till morning. It was not a matter we ever discussed because although my husband was a very forceful man as well as a very successful one, he was also a very shy man, and there were certain things he didn't feel comfortable talking about even to me. When we traveled, however, it was a different story because in hotels and on ocean liners we often found ourselves sharing a room, and it always gave me a wonderful sense of peace to wake up in the dark and hear the sound of his breathing.

"It was once in London when we were staying at the Goring, I think, that this unforgettable thing happened. Why on earth am I telling you about it? I think it must be that remembering Colin and our hut in the woods brought it to mind. And how I wept at that football game when I caught a glimpse of the girl I once had been.

"We had a charming little suite looking down into the garden they have in back. We had often stayed there before so the manager had a vase of lovely white roses and a basket of fresh fruit waiting for us when we arrived. Well, one night when it came time for bed, Harold went into the bathroom as he always did to put on his pajamas, but I was already tucked in with my book so he didn't bother to shut the door tight and left it just enough ajar so that when I happened to glance up from whatever I was reading, I could see him. He was standing in front of the bathroom mirror brushing his teeth, and he had nothing on except his bedroom slippers. I had never seen him naked before, and then, just for an instant, our eyes met in the mirror. Such a little thing it was, but oh what an unforgettable thing! And that was not the end of it.

"The next night I was the one who left the bathroom door ajar, only in my case it was on purpose. I didn't have the courage to catch his eye in the mirror the way he had mine, but I knew he could see me standing there with not a stitch on, and I remember how I didn't feel embarrassed or ashamed the way I would have thought because what I was doing was trying to give him something as precious as what I had been given the night before. It was never, never, spoken of between us—my dear, he would have absolutely died—but it did not have to be spoken. It was part of what I could see in his eyes after he lost the power to speak.

"I was a virgin the day Harold Conover married me, and I was a virgin the day he died.

"And I am quite certain that Harold Conover was a virgin too."

Dickens's Christmas Carol

Charles Dickens wrote his *Christmas Carol* in less than two months—October–November 1843—and apparently in a fine frenzy. "With what a strange mastery it seized him for itself," his old friend and biographer John Forster wrote. "How he wept over it, and laughed, and wept again, and excited himself to an extraordinary degree, and how he walked thinking of it fifteen and twenty miles about the black streets of London, many and many a night after all sober folks had gone to bed. And when it was done, as he told our friend Mr. Felton in America, he let himself loose like a madman."

But his frenzy by no means led him to rush it through as you might think. On the contrary, it is clear that he took unusual pains with it, and the manuscript is cluttered with deletions and corrections and many pages entirely rewritten as though he knew he was onto something special and wanted to make sure he got it down exactly right. Nor did his pains end with the writing alone but extended to the book's production as well. Chapman and Hall were publishing it on commission so it was out of his own pocket that Dickens paid for what turned out to be the most expensive format of any of the books he ever wrote, insisting that it have gilt edges and a title page printed in red and blue with colored endpapers and four richly hand-colored illustrations by John Leech showing old Fezziwig's ball, Marley's ghost, the Ghost of Christmas present with a crown of green mistletoe on his head, and finally Scrooge himself kneeling at his own lonely grave with his face buried in his hands.

When publication finally took place, just before Christmas he gave a great party to celebrate with many children on hand as well as his own. His friend Macready the actor couldn't attend because he was off on tour in America, so Dickens wrote him a description of it. Mrs. Macready was there, he said, looking "brilliant, blooming, young, and handsome," as she and Dickens danced "a country dance" together, and then he and Forster performed a number of magic tricks. "A plum pudding," he continued, "was produced from an empty saucepan, held over a blazing fire kindled in Stanfield's hat without damage to the lining, [and] a box of bran was changed into a live guinea-pig, which ran between my godchild's feet, and was the cause of such a shrill uproar and clapping of hands that you might have heard it (and I daresay did) in America."

Thomas Carlyle's wife Jane was another one of the guests, and her account in a letter to some relative is a forest of exclamation points and underlinings. "Dickens and Forster," she wrote, "above all exerted themselves till the perspiration was pouring down and they seemed *drunk* with their efforts. Only think of that excellent Dickens playing the *conjuror* for one whole hour—the *best* conjuror I ever saw. . . . Then the dancing . . . the gigantic Thackeray &c &c all capering like *Maenades!* . . . *after supper* when we were all madder than ever with the pulling of crackers, the drinking of champagne, and the making of speeches, a universal country dance was proposed— and Forster *seizing me around the waist,* whirled me into the thick of it, and *made* me dance like a person in the tread-mill who must move forward or be crushed to death! Once I cried out, 'Oh for the love of Heaven let me go! You are going to dash my brains out against the folding doors!' 'Your *brains!*' he answered, 'who cares about your brains *here? Let them go!*'"

Dickens and Forster, Mrs. Macready and Mrs. Carlyle, William Makepeace Thackeray and heaven only knows who all else—it is tempting to imagine Victoria herself joining in on the fun with the Prince Consort in tow, not to mention Disraeli and Palmerston, Lord Tennyson and Mr. Browning and Anthony Trollope with his whiskers flying, maybe even the Duke of Wellington in his old age, and whoever else you can think of including everybody who in all the years that have gone by since that distant day have found the *Christmas Carol* a cause for joyous celebration. It is Dickens's undoubted masterpiece and in its own way an extracanonical Gospel. Every year I watch the great 1951 film version of it starring Alastair Sim as Scrooge with my face bathed in tears.

Family Poems

Great-grandfather

Grandfather Kuhn

Mattie Poor

The Four Aunts

Uncle George

The Great-uncles

Aunt Doozie

Kaki

The Cousins

Florida

Miriam

Johnny

Lawrenceville Fiftieth Reunion

Great-grandfather

My great-grandfather Adam Kuhn sold hardware, harness,
and feed in Clarion County though even in sleeve guards
and eyeshade he looked more a judge in his handsome beard
and starched collar with only his sly little eyes full of secrets
to give the whole show away.

His two sons and two daughters helped with his farm.
His soft-spoken wife named Emily revered him as he
revered her. After thanking the Lord at meals for the food
He'd provided, he would look at her plate and say, "Emmy.
     What's that?
Don't eat it. It might be pizon."

They tell that a friend once said, "Adam, how about you
and me going halves on a store where nothing costs more
than a nickel or dime. It might just catch on," and he called
it a damn fool idea and turned him down flat. Woolworth,
it seems, was the name of the friend.

Every so often he'd be gone when they woke in the morning
and might not return for as much as a week, but never
did one of them ask where he'd been and not once did he tell.
He survived to be almost a hundred, his wife long since
     dead,
and moved into my grandfather's house

where he'd run up the steep gravel drive like a rabbit to keep
himself trim, was a patent medicine addict and squirreled
penny candy under his bed. His pet was my blue-eyed

mother and from each of his trips he would bring her some
    heart-shaped
bauble she kept in a velvet-lined

box that years later she lost on a train to be left
brokenhearted. Where did he go on his trips? Maybe no
    place
at all, maybe just sat on the roof with his beautiful
beard and a bagful of ointments and tonics
and gumdrops, and glorified God.

Grandfather Kuhn

My grandfather wore his hat in the house,
a straw that rode low on his brow crowding
his jellybean mole and smudged specs,
his nose and scruffy moustache hitched high
as he cocked one ear to the war news, read *Life*,
or scratched out in an indecipherable hand
endless letters. He let my grandmother do all
the talking, he admired her so—how only
that day she'd been collared on Trade Street by Mrs.
Scruggs Brown, who spent twenty-five minutes on ways
To cook onions, a brother who'd somehow mislaid
Both his kidneys, and her plan to adopt twelve children,
Most of them boys, when the time seemed right.
"Strong men run for cover when she comes into view,"
my grandmother said, "but in fur piece and pearls
she's quick on the trigger as Jesse James."
My grandmother's words silvered the air
like her Chesterfield's haze while out of the straw
of those Tryon days—so at loose ends we were,
so down on our luck—she spun gold, showed how even
the worst, such as run-ins on Trade Street with Mrs.
Scruggs Brown, could be turned into treasure.

My grandfather must have had tales to tell too,
but he gave us only a glimpse now and then
when his guard was down. Jane Cavan, for instance,
the one he'd adored above all, his Irish
grandmother, though why he adored her he never
explained, just her name: "Jane Cavan, now there

Was a corker!" He kept the rest under his hat,
whatever she'd been to him back as a boy
in Clarion County where H.A., his bully

brother, told him his feet weren't mates
and he'd have to take gumsquirt and fewfew to fix them,
whatever that was. In her photos their mother
looked owl-like and dim with her great moist gaze
and crimped hair. Their bearded father
had the face of a sage and the sly, small eyes
of a fox

      Shy Grandfather, tell of the sky-blue-
eyed boy you were growing up, tell of the Honorable
D. J. Neff of Altoona, the judge you read law with,
your practice in Knoxville, and meeting a dark
slender girl who rode horseback, taught school,
and told you her weight, ninety-nine, was the weight
of a witch. When you made her your wife,
did Jane Cavan and she ever meet, those two women
you loved? Did she balk when you took her to Pittsburgh
along with the babies to go into coal
with H.A., whom she always despised for perpetually
putting you down with his fancy degrees
and superior airs. "Wilson, pass me
the H 2 0," he intoned once at dinner,
and my grandmother: "Wilson, please pass
the H 2 0 to the FO 2 L."

———

How did it feel when you struck it rich
and moved to a house not a stone's throw from Andy
Mellon's with car and chauffeur, a brick terrace,
a piano my grandmother played with one finger
as the sun flooded in through French windows, a girl
in a portrait holding a flower, a Chinese
vase tall as a child? I remember
the library's hush and the books behind glass,
the white staircase that curved to a landing, then angled
up to the mystery of maids' rooms and attics,
the front hall's Indian carpet a dizzying
distance below.

               Houses had only one
phone then, and yours was kept in a closet
under the stairs where twice in her life
my grandmother saw you emerge with the news
you had lost your shirt. First came the Crash
which left you at least the big house and one maid,
but then there were oil wells found out to be only
dry holes plus the money you sank in Rube Goldberg
contraptions, especially the ones of a fast-talking
Swiss who promised you millions till finally
you had to abandon the Mellons, the Marmon
and driver, the flowering horse chestnuts, and limped
down to Tryon where for more than ten years you tried
to recoup till at last you let go and took
to wearing your hat in the house and writing
those letters that no one who got them could read.

———

Mag Zogbaum, my grandmother said, was leaving
the Captain to search for a government job
on the strength of the five foreign tongues she claimed
she could speak like a native, rigged out in a peacock
blue hat run up from an evening dress belt
and her face painted Easter egg bright. If you asked her
for cocktails she always left early, sweeping
leftover hors d'oeuvres into a bag
to take home for supper for her and the Captain.
With her coppery braid wreathed round her head
like a heavily powdered and doorknob-chinned Guinevere
out of Burne-Jones, she appeared in a host
of my grandmother's tales along with the little
Sassoons, who like British sparrows chirped
at their guests both at once, Clifton Murphy with his acid
tongue and his taste for Boy Scouts, not to mention
the lady whose astral body went fishing
at night, and old Dr. Law who shot cats.
Such was the Tryon world as my grandmother
spun it like one of the socks she was endlessly
knitting, her hair in a bun and her face
like the mottled page of an old book.

My grandfather listened, took walks in the woods
with his stick and yellow old Minnie, read Sandburg's
Lincoln, kept track of the war. But his memories
back to the first term of Grant of how it had been
to be him, of Jane Cavan, of losing a fortune

twice, he spoke not a word of and nobody
asked. Years later I heard that during
the First World War when his coal mines were running
full tilt and the governor put him in charge
of West Pennsylvania's fuel and his face every day
in the papers, a lady stepped forth whom the tabloids
billed as The Stolen Princess with claims
he had done her wrong. But in time it somehow
blew over and was never mentioned again.

Grandfather, mention it now. Was she pretty
and young? Was it only a fling or true love?
Sitting there in your hat, did you think of her ever?
Remember her name? What did my grandmother
say? Your children? If I'd ever dared ask
years later, would you even have known what I meant?
Would your shaggy-browed, mild blue eyes have caught fire,
forced at last to see who I was as at last
I saw you, hanging on to your words as I'd always
Hung on to your wife's?

                    Her tales and your silence,
were they both of them ways to keep hidden the time
when, more than a fortune, you almost lost all
that you were to each other and also to me
who for going on eighty-one years have never
forgotten the peace of your house or my love?

Mattie Poor

Mattie Poor fell in love
in the Washington house
of the great Clara Barton
her much older cousin
who summoned her down
from New England to help
with the secret rolls
that were smuggled to her
of the Union prisoners
dead and buried
at Andersonville
printing their names
in the papers so kin
might at last learn their fate
and locate their graves.

Letters came in
by the cartload and Mattie
fresh from Augusta
Maine where she taught
piano and voice
was given the task
of replying along
with a gallant young Swiss
who had fought for the North
and been found close to death
by Miss Barton herself
so touching her heart
with his sad brown eyes

and the ocean he'd crossed
to help free the slaves
that when he was well
she invited him in
like a twenty years younger

brother and gave him
the run of the house
and threw back her head
and laughed when in time
on his knees he asked her
to marry.

When poor Mattie Poor
arrived knowing nothing
of this he knelt down
once more only this time
to her and she was
so struck by his sad
brown eyes and his curly
beard that she answered him
yes and then bore him
a daughter and a few months
later was dead
of consumption to be laid
in an unmarked grave
in the Barton plot
in North Oxford Mass
leaving only a packet

of letters too faded
to read and the daughter
who lived to be ninety
and the brightest star
in her octogenarian
grandson's sky
to this day.

The Four Aunts

Aunt Lynne had the purr of a duchess, a mole's little eyes.
If something dismayed her or caused her surprise,
She wriggled her fingers in front of her nose
Like roseworms defending the heart of the rose.

Aunt Olga's eyes were glacier blue, her hair cobweb thin,
She raised Shetland ponies, had a taste for gin.
She could stare down a bishop, outswear a groom.
If your views didn't please her, you soon left the room.

Aunt Elspeth died young. How on earth could it be?
She was jolly and strong, the mother of three.
But once under ether something went wrong,
And too soon they forgot her like the words of a song.

Aunt Magda's voice was sharp as a pin.
Her malice was gratis, she sinned just to sin.
Struck dumb by a stroke, she spoke never again
But each time she broke wind, clucked for joy like a hen.

Uncle George

Not knowing the rear door was open,
he sheared it off at the hinge
backing out of the four-car garage
with my grandmother there at his side,
his mother-in-law, his tennis racket
between them. "Dear boy, it can surely
be mended," she said as he grabbed
the racket in both of his hands
and used it to batter the Packard
to death with her still inside,
her cigarette in a white paper holder,
the smoke drifting out where the door
had once been. He mellowed in time,
but I once saw him hurl a fire screen
the whole length of a room
for not standing straight, heard him
threaten to punch my grandfather's nose
on a matter of taxes.

He was fourteen years old walking off
demerits at Choate when they told him
the S.S. *Titanic* had sunk with his parents
and sister aboard coming home,
and he went to New York to meet
the survivors not knowing which
of the three would get off if any.
It was only his father who failed to,
and for more than a year they kept thinking
someday the doorbell would ring

and he would be there in his pince-nez
and Saville Row clothes, fished out
by some freighter or smack bound somewhere.

In time he went bald with a fringe
and a close-cropped moustache to cover
an iceboating scar from his youth
and retired from Wall Street to live
in the South, where he drew up and built
for himself and my aunt a house
so many admired he made
a career building houses for friends
and became a success. My aunt
to fight ire with ire, as my grandmother
said, once threw every stitch
he owned out the window and tore
all his Kodachrome slides to bits,
and I think he enjoyed it as giving
him leave to go on, like an iceberg,
attacking the world for sailing
the first-class travelers as well
as the steerage to darkness and doom.

The Great-uncles

My great-uncles Alwin and Herman, my grandfather's
Pint-sized bachelor brothers
From Brooklyn,

Came with their derby hats and cigars
On Christmas Day only. If they'd ever
Shown up

In their long fur coats on Groundhog Day, say,
Would they have packed them off
To the zoo?

Maybe baked them into a pie fully dressed
Though bowlers taste bitter and stogies
Cause gas?

Aunt Doozie

Because she was stepping out later, Aunt Doozie dressed
To the nines for her trip to the New York World's Fair one hot
Afternoon of July '39 taking Tommy and Nancy,
Her children, and Freddy, their cousin, all under fourteen.

She wore a pink suit with white beads big as grapes and
        white earrings,
Sheer silk stockings, spike heels, and a rather large hat that
        dipped
Over one ear with some sort of feather that curled down in
        back.
She didn't need rouge but patted some on for good measure.

Freddy's father had died only three years before but already
He'd all but forgotten his face and his voice and since nobody
Spoke of him, neither did he, so "the World of Tomorrow,"
The theme of the Fair, sounded fine to him who had no

Yesterday to speak of. The first thing they saw was the General
Motors Exhibit where in six hundred moving chairs
With loudspeakers they gave you a tour of the U.S. to come
Where the seven-lane roads plus the absence of slums and
        abundance

Of parks seemed to promise a heaven on earth in twenty
Years time, and Aunt Doozie said, "Children, just think how
        lucky
We are that if nothing goes wrong we'll all of us live
To see it!" which made Freddy think for a moment of dying.

When they reached the Lagoon of Nations, she asked a
          young black
If he'd take a shot of them all with her Brownie, then lined
Them up with the sun in their eyes and said, "Children, isn't
It grand to see all these countries' flags and pavilions

So peaceful together? It's a shame the Germans aren't here
But someday they'll come, just you wait. Nancy, don't squint,
And Tommy, stop squirming. Now all of you look at the
          camera.
Say cheese!" The quarter she offered the black he turned down.

What Nancy liked best was the Liberty Bell reproduced
By Japan in silver all studded with hundreds of diamonds
And pearls. What caught Freddy's eye was the capsule sunk
Fifty feet in the ground and filled with mementos to dig up

Again in five thousand years so that no one would ever
Forget us, our faces, our voices, the things that we did
In our day but would always remember we once were alive,
Even the ones hardly anyone now remembered.

"It says in the Bible a thousand years in God's sight
Aren't worth squat," said Aunt Doozie, "but still it's amazing
          to think
Of people so long after us standing here. What clothes
Will they wear? Will they even have bodies like ours?"

"Maybe they'll have six legs each," Tommy said, and Freddy,

"Or no legs at all, just huge heads stuffed with brains." Nancy
Wanted to go where the fun was, the dodgem cars, loop-the-
        loops,
Freak shows, a lady dressed only in grapes with pigeons

That pecked them off one by one, and the Parachute Jump
That Tommy and Nancy rode into the sky while Aunt Doozie
And Freddy watched from below. Aunt Doozie alone
Had the guts for the next—a great wheel from the end of
        whose spokes

Hung Buck Rogers rockets that not only spun with the wheel
In a circle but also spun, each by itself, end
Over end, at breathtaking speeds. Climbing aboard
Wasn't easy, but they strapped her in finally, latching the door,

While the children, their hearts in their mouths, watched as
        they would
A beheading till finally it came to a stop and Aunt Doozie
Crawled out. Her hat was down over her eyes and the feather
Missing. One French heel was gone. One stocking was down

To her knee and the other in tatters. The red of her rouge
Was all over her face. Was she having a stroke? Was she
        laughing?
Maybe crying? The children weren't sure. Speechless, she
        limped
On her one good heel to where they were standing and
        hugged them.

"Oh children!" she gasped. "I've wet myself. Does it show?
I've lost a white earring. I'm afraid I'm about to be sick.
All this Trylon and Perisphere hoopla is bosh. This World
Of Tomorrow's a joke. The world's in as crazy a mess

As this whole crazy place. There may never be a tomorrow.
I was crazy to bring you. I'm sorry. It's time to go home."
Tommy gave her his Coke and Nancy a hankie for dabbing
Her tears till at last she was back on her feet and laughing.

But Freddy never forgot her terror and grief
And anger, her pink suit in ruins. If the world could do that
To Aunt Doozie, they were none of them safe. For the rest of
        the Fair
He kept his eyes shut to see how it would be to be dead.

Kaki

Me and my shadow walking down
the avenue, down past the foot of the park,
past the sparrows scrambling for crumbs, the pigeons,
the shallow basin of rain in the arms

of the naked lady, the shining angel
holding the General's bridle, the hacks
at the Plaza entrance dozing in harness,
their noses in oats, the black umbrellas

of doormen, and on down past Bonwit's and Lizzie
Arden's red door to the doors of Saint Patrick's
that only my shadow can enter these days
where I used to see poor old biddies telling

their beads. At ninety I haven't a soul
to tell anything, alone in my chair feeling lonely,
the *Daily News* on my old biddy knees.
Only my shadow can walk still.

We have parted ways, my shadow and me.
I am the last rose of summer, the dark
at the end of the tunnel. Remember me, please,
to the naked lady. Kiss the foot of the park.

The Cousins

In their grandmother's empty apartment, the blinds
drawn for summer, the furniture sheeted.
The night

they watched Armstrong step down on the empty moon,
then skinnydipped in the dark, in the dark
pool.

On spring afternoons, off at school, walking deep
in the woods, stretching out in the cool
of some tree

side by side. Whatever they touched turned to gold.
They turned each other to gold,
their shoulders

touching. There was never a soul they told,
hardly even each other.
Growing old,

with their wives, they met mostly like strangers, like ghosts
keeping folded in silence the treasure
they'd lost.

Florida

Because it is blue where the sea lies,
Because of the sand, how it gives under your feet or
          gives hardly at all,
Because of the flatness allowing your eye to travel as
          far as the lip of the world,
I forgive it the terrible malls,
I forgive it Walt Disney and Flagler,
I forgive it the armadillo dead by the
          side of the road.

Because of the malls more marvelous far than
          museums,
I forgive it the hurricane's havoc, the ravening shark, the
          Portuguese man-of-war.

Because of the Portuguese man-of-war's purple and
          gentian blue bladder,
I forgive it the in and out of the tides that remind me of
          life, remind me of death.

Because of its porpoise smile,
Because its pelicans fly not much better than I would
          fly if I were a bird,
I dare ask its forgiveness for us being us,
Dare walk on its sands with my eyes closed,
Dare lie like a child in the lap of its sea.

Miriam

Her house was a three-year-old's drawing
of a house—two windows on the second floor
and two below to flank the door.
On the porch a pair of supermarket tube
and webbing chairs in case a guest or two
dropped by plus one where she could lean way back,
a coverlet across her knees when fall
was in the air or she felt ill.

The shades she always kept exactly so,
the ones above just low
enough to hide her on her way to bed,
the ones below up high to let
some daylight in. Now that the house is empty
as a drum, they're every whichway
like an old drunk's stare,
and somebody's pinched the supermarket chairs.

Sweet Jesus, forgive me all the days I spotted
her in one of them and slunk behind the trees
across the street. A caller on her porch
for all to see she would have rated
with her trip to England on a plane,
or winning first prize for her grapenut pie,
or the day that she retired from the Inn
and they gave her a purple orchid on a pin.

Or a nice boy asking her to dance,

or being voted president of her class,
or some spring morning with her room all warm
and sunlit waking up in Spencer Tracy's arms.

Johnny

He held the giraffe
so long in his delicate
hand he forgot
the giraffe-shaped hole
forgot where he was
who he was if he knew
like a president signing
a bill into law
he placed it at last
upside down first
then straight where it went
the place it belonged
tightening his lips
in disdain like the only
man in a room
full of children

his window gave out
on the waterway windsurfing
boys girls all gold
in bikinis a pelican
perched on the dock
if anyone opened
the door his lament
rose at the end
to the shrill of Oedipus
blinded a cow
giving birth
they lowered him into

the pool in a harness
hoisted him into
a van in his chair
drove him anywhere miles

a nurse said he grasped
almost all that he heard
said once in the dark
he woke with his father's
name on his lips
some line from a song
sometimes he reached out his hand
to whoever was there
to strangers to touch them
please he said please

sometimes he turned
his slow head with a smile
that could break your heart
break the pane in the window
let in the water
the sky the pelican
robed like a prince
like a shining prince
like a shining.

Lawrenceville Fiftieth Reunion

In June of '43 out on the lawn
In front of Dickinson, the sunlight scattering gold
Down through the tall leaves overhead and all
The step- and grand- and just plain parents, friends,
And hangers-on in rows of folding chairs,
I read the poem I'd labored on for days
Of which old Charlie Raymond, head cocked sideways,
Said when he first checked it over, "Fred,
I think you can do better." Maybe so,
But I decided that I'd let not well enough
Alone and when the time came read it anyhow
Including one sizzling sibillance I'd cribbed from Conrad
Aiken—"the secret softness of the silent snow."
I was a pimply, pale sixteen. My hair
Was parted in the middle and Vitalissed down.
Except for the part worn on my sleeve, my heart
Was in my mouth. Allan Heely, Jordan
Churchill, Hans Rastede—all the Olympians
Were there, plus pretty girls in pageboy bobs,
Giant industrialists in double-breasted suits,
And legendary moms. The PA system
Made my voice a stranger's as I read:
"Today begins so soon to be tomorrow,
And these my words will be so soon a piece
Of yesterday, that were it not that sorrow
Is a useless thing, I would be sad and cease
To live the present and become the past."
End quote.
Pa Raymond had it right, no doubt.

I could have honed it up a bit and toned
It down, improved a rhyme or two, and yet,
In those first lines at least, the callow youth
I was spoke simple truth. Not just his words
But that whole world of nineteen forty-three
Got buried deep in yesterdays in no time flat,
And we who've lived to tell the tale are boys
No more but rich men, poor men, beggars, thieves,
And thieved, ourselves, of much that seemed for keeps:
Pop Bussom jerking jiggers, Pete Petrone
Collecting shoes from house to house to shine,
Ted Keller belting out the chapel chimes
Or rising from the organ pit to pull
His nose and say the next piece was by Bach.
       Does the soggy-washrag, Walker Gordon smell
Still drift at dawn across the golf course greens?
In those days no one dreamed that cigarettes
Did worse than cut your wind. Knowing now
The cut is to the quick, do seniors puff
Them still out on the Esplanade at dusk?
Do any act—on stage or off—like Barry Doig?
Or rack up grades the way Bill Umstattd did?
Ham Neely, A. P. Loening, J. P. Ross—
Do current models come at all like those?
Are any nowadays Miranda-suave or Lever
Stewart–full-of-beans or Jimmy Merrill–bright?
Do they make end runs like Johnny Grymes or write
Long, moonstruck letters to the girl back home
When these days there are girls galore right here?

Is it only a dream that we wore coats and ties
To class and rose when masters came into the room?
Can the fifty-year reuners our Commencement
Spring, who came here then as we come now,
Have been the class of *eighteen* ninety-three?
Was there a time when at the movie's end
They played the national anthem and we stood
With lump in throat because the war was on,
America was beautiful still, and we had cause
To think our lives would soon be up for grabs?
Can anybody watch those movies that we saw—
Ninotchka, Casablanca, In Which We Serve—
Without a tear or two for all that innocence
Lost, for all that world which, once the fight
We fought to save it ended, ended too
As did some precious part of us as well
Who, even though we lived to tell the tale,
Have never been so full of life again?
            That golden June just half a century gone . . .
The mothers' tasseled programs used for fans . . .
The hazy air, the smell of new-cut grass . . .
Mem Hall crouched romanesquely like a toad . . .
The Circle Houses dozing in the shade . . .
Starched shirts and seersucker wilting . . . Memories fade
And then go bright again like sun through leaves.
I finished up my poem like this. I said,
"Remember too that life is very good,
And that to live is better than to die,"
And all in all I'd say so still though sixty-

Six is not so sure as sweet sixteen
What life and death are all about. Suppose
We *lose* less, dying, than we *find*. Who knows?
Life's good, for sure, but would we choose to live
Forever if we could? Or might that seem
Like twilight never deepening into dark,
Like never calling it a day, and letting
Go, and lying down to sleep. "Life should
Be wondered at," I said, "not understood,"
As if I thought there was a choice, then said,
"Remember love," as if we might forget.

      Our families driving down to sit in Edith's
Varnished pews and clap while Allan Heely
Read our names with some trustee to deal
Diplomas out. The pals who signed our Olla Pods.
The faculty with all its superstars, its odds
And ends. The coffee hours to which we came
With Pattie always knowing all our names
Just like Pat Coughlin with his pushbroom. Friends
We had who didn't live to be old men
Like us.

      Remember *Love?* For starters try
Remembering *back*. God bless them all. Goodbye.